SILO

SILO

THE ZERO WASTE BLUEPRINT

A FOOD SYSTEM FOR THE FUTURE

DOUGLAS MCMASTER

Leaping Hare Press

First published in the UK in 2019 by
Leaping Hare Press
An imprint of The Quarto Group
1 Triptych Place, 2nd Floor, London,
SE1 9SH, United Kingdom
T (0)20 7700 6700 **F** (0)20 7700 8066
www.Quarto.com

British Library Cataloguing-in-
Publication Data
A catalogue record for this book is
available from the British Library.

ISBN: 978-1-78240-613-6

This book was conceived, designed
and produced by
Leaping Hare Press
1 Triptych Place, 2nd Floor, London,
SE1 9SH, United Kingdom

Publisher Susan Kelly
Editorial Director Tom Kitch
Commissioning Editor Monica Perdoni
Project Editor Caroline Earle
Designer Michael Whitehead
Original Concept Design Studio Makgill
Photography Xavier D. Buendia,
Douglas McMaster
Illustrations Giacomo Bufarini – RUN,
Douglas McMaster, StudioLewis

Printed in Bosnia and Herzegovina

10 9 8 7

CONTENTS

MOTIVE 16
THE CIRCUMSTANCES
THAT MOTIVATED SILO

IDEAS 46
THE THEORETICAL OVERVIEW
OF SILO'S SYSTEMS AND IDEAS

FORMULA 90
THE EXECUTION OF THE PRODUCT TRUE TO THE IDEAS

NO CONCLUSION 150
WHAT WE HAVE LEARNED

WORDS FROM THE TRIBE

THE PLANET NEEDS THIS BOOK – SO SAY THE PIONEERS, THE VINDICATORS AND THE MAVERICKS

'I've always said that it's in a chef's DNA to utilize what would otherwise be thrown away. We are hardwired to take the uncoveted and make it delicious. But Doug McMaster is on another level entirely – he is doing some of the most thorough and thoughtful work on food waste today. This book gives you more than a glimpse into his mind. It provides a much needed roadmap for a future of limited resources and growing demands.'

Dan Barber, Chef and Co-owner
Blue Hill at Stone Barns

'This is a book I cannot wait to dive into. Doug and Silo have been a strong source of inspiration for the culture that we have created around this way of thinking at Amass. The ideas and principles that are put forth in this book should be a playbook that the whole industry strives to emulate.'

Matthew Orlando, Head Chef/Owner
Amass Restaurant, Copenhagen

'The universe needs people that think and act like Dougie.'

Lee Tiernan, Head Chef
Black Axe Mangal, London

'When facing a dire and uncertain future with immediate climatic changes our habits often impede us from making any radical change. Our industry and our planet need pioneers like Doug McMaster to challenge those habits and the ways we look at our daily work. The way Silo is spearheading the Zero Waste movement is an inspiration to us professional chefs and, with this book, will hopefully inspire you to reconsider your footprint, your waste and your cooking.'

Christian F. Puglisi, Co-owner
Relæ Copenhagen

'There are some people who initiate ideas, and then there are some mavericks that refuse to stand still, or simply accept a spotlight of a fading fame; Doug is very much the second of these. Not only did he challenge conventions and prove something to the world (namely that sustainability was not only crucial, but that it could be delicious, exciting, honest and everyday), but he refused to sit still with it. This book is what the world has needed; not a passion project or a curiosity, a genuine blueprint for how we can all do better and how we can use food and drink to improve our world. To say this is crucial, and to say I'm excited is an understatement!'

Ryan Chetiyawardana, 'Mr Lyan',
Owner, *Super Lyan*/Co-owner, *Cub, London*

THIS IS NOT A COOKBOOK

THERE ARE A LOT OF COOKBOOKS IN THE WORLD, THIS IS NOT ANOTHER. IT'S DESIGNED TO BE PICKED UP FOR A SHORT TIME, BUT ALSO FOR A LONG TIME.

Each page is its own little ecosystem that can survive on its own, be it in the form of literature, diagrams, photography or illustration. That said, 'everything is connected', a web of life serving one big system = Zero Waste.

Silo is a restaurant that doesn't have a bin: from that simple limitation grows a big tree. At the very tip of the tree is the product. Instead of focusing on just the product, we're looking at the whole tree, beginning with the roots and following it all the way to the bright shiny leaves.

What's crucial for Silo is that the product represents the process, because the process represents the nature that feeds it. If you compose a bad system you yield bad food; however, a good system yields good food. Knowing the system from the point of nature presents a greater level of control, tethering ingredients straight from their habitat.

We will present a different approach to recipes; we're not doing recipes at all. Rather, a whole view of how the food feeds from the system. It's important because it's a real life example of sustainability – one that works economically, is delicious and creates Zero Waste. It's backed up with formulas that encourage intuition. Less robot cooking and more wizard skills.

OH, AND KEEP AN OPEN MIND, YOU'LL NEED IT.

'THERE COMES A POINT
WHERE WE NEED TO STOP
JUST PULLING PEOPLE
OUT OF THE RIVER.
WE NEED TO GO UPSTREAM
AND FIND OUT WHY THEY'RE
FALLING IN.'

DESMOND TUTU

1

MOTIVE

THE PEASANT AND THE PROPHET

OVER A DECADE AGO, BEFORE SILO WAS BORN, I DROPPED OUT OF SCHOOL. I DIDN'T LIKE SCHOOL: I'M DYSLEXIC, DYSCALCULIC, DYS-EVERYTHING.

I don't take well to being told what to do. As soon as somebody tells me what to do, I want to do the opposite. I fell out of school at 16 and fell into a kitchen; it was the only place that would have me. It's the same story for a lot of chefs.

Kitchens are pretty unruly places, full of anarchy and chaos. The life of a chef is similar to the life of a pirate – there are rules and discipline, but there is also the freedom to express yourself and be an individual. I fell in love with the kitchens. I was used to being in classrooms, being told what to do and being miserable. Kitchens felt free. I liked the loud music and wild language. You still had to be on time and achieve whatever's needed of you that day, but not at the expense of your soul. I felt like I'd woken up, I'd found my tribe. I didn't know it then, but I had a chip on my shoulder; an insatiable need to work at the best restaurants, make my CV shine, wear those big names like medals – the chip demanded it.

I found guidance in the 'almighty guide' and embarked on a gruelling stint through the Michelin-starred citadels of the North. After a few years, my youthful resolve began succumbing to the anarchy, a friend convinced me to leave the hallowed shrines of the North and come work at Fergus Henderson's St John Bread and Wine in London. The St John restaurants were an anomaly in the landscape of gastronomy, not such an obvious beauty, hard to decipher for the uninitiated. I was a 20-year-old lad who thought St John was a joke. Where were the neat dots? The foam? The sous vide? I must have been insufferable. However, working there very quickly changed my perspective.

The chefs at St John were much older, less aggressive and altogether out of tune with everything I knew; only the chef whites were recognizable. James, the head chef, was the first significant Silo influencer. While working in this temple galvanized with identity, he was a force of his own. His values were sage and confident, not always in tune with his surroundings. He was a very nice chap, we'd talk for hours about food around the world, his thoughts were sophisticated and intelligent, I ate up every word. However, there was James the diplomat and James the bloodthirsty knight. If I disobeyed his formula, intentionally or not, there were fierce consequences; rage would ensue, which would be impossible for me to shrug off.

James and I would work services that I'll remember forever. A terrified peasant and crazed prophet going into battle – unprepared, unarmed with impossible odds, destined to suffer. I crumbled in every battle, I was useless. However, while I was getting munched up by the outnumbering horde, James revelled in it: he was thirsty for action and knew he was unstoppable. The other chefs that worked with James told a very different story, apparently the wrath was bottled up. This was hard to stomach. I'd like to think he saw something in me, he wanted me to learn the hard way, that through suffering I would become stronger.

Maybe not, maybe I was that bad.

Head chefs are so often barbaric; the surge of power in such a volatile environment is intoxicated by ego. James wasn't like most chefs. While ego is part of us all, he was possessed by his own code. This wasn't a job for him, he cooked with a purpose – there was something he saw on the horizon and he was moving directly towards that – nobody was going to get in his way.

It was the training (and other subliminalities) I received at St John that led me to trust in 'magical intuition'. When rid of safety measures, you only have your instincts to survive. St John taught me to cook for a reason: respect the produce, banish all that is superfluous, cook whole food, cherish the whole beast, obey the seasons. It felt natural, honest, and we were cooking for an honourable idea.

I AM NOT THE CHOSEN ONE

AS A TEENAGER, I WAS DECLARED 'DUMB'. I WAS TOLD SO BY THE OTHER KIDS AND THE TEACHERS, AND I FELT IT.

It wasn't just the inexperience; I was hopeless, I had no confidence, there was so much I didn't know.

One day, when I was working at St John, I received an email to participate in a national cooking competition. I thought, 'There is nothing to lose.' Over 1,400 applicants entered, I was told later. After rigorous culinary gatherings, I was chosen with four others for the final showdown. This competition was the BBC Young Chef of the Year. There I was, a 21-year-old with no discernible achievements, and I was going to be cooking on national TV. Here we were, kids barely in our 20s, dropped into a new reality, an army of cameras stalking our every twitch. The format of these competitions go for telegenic thrills: we had to cook against near-impossible odds, face challenges that the judges themselves would trip over.

Thankfully, it was on this day that a switch suddenly flipped for me. It's like the part in *The Matrix* when Keanu Reeves dramatically pauses and says: 'I KNOW KUNG FU.' You see, up until this point I had so little confidence; I had worked for some really amazing restaurants but had always remained the grunt of the kitchen.

The first challenge of the competition was to cook four egg dishes in 30 minutes: boiled egg and soldiers, poached salmon and hollandaise, steak with bearnaise, and a lemon soufflé. I remember a rush of fear, anxiety, panic; so much that I felt paralysed. I could see all the other chefs racing around. I was overwhelmed, riddled with doubt. All of a sudden, it went quiet.

Then it came, a deep breath, a gift from the gods. It was as if the deep breath cleared all emotion from my mind. Sound returned, and I knew what to do. As Keanu started deflecting the strikes of Agent Smith with ease, I started cooking. It all started making perfect sense: I KNOW HOW TO COOK. I realized, with just four minutes remaining, that I hadn't started on the soufflé. Again, I collected myself in a breath, and without fear the ingredients came together with a clear mind. I closed the oven door just as the timer stopped. The judges were chipper, impressed with what they could see, but, 'Where is the soufflé?' It had finished cooking at that exact moment and I pulled it out to the judges' huzzah. It was as if I knew it would take them three minutes to review my first three dishes – it made great television!

I ended up winning the competition. Blood, guts, failures and now, finally, a taste of glory. I had achieved what I thought meant 'success'. It was a feeling of ecstasy that went on for days. Unfortunately, that feeling wore off. A few days later I remember thinking, 'Now what?' This was my first existential crisis. Why do I still feel empty? How do I feel fulfilment? What does it all mean? The high of winning a competition like that leaves you needing more, it's addictive. I needed more success, but where would I find it? What would it cost?

It's common to want what others want. I wanted to be the best chef, now I wanted to own my own restaurant. Furthermore, I wanted it to mean something, like St John. Before St John, I'd been cooking for 'the almighty guide', a purpose simply orbiting 'excellence'. Rabid chefs in a barren landscape, marching towards the oasis, a place known as 'perfection'.

In an effort to go the other way, I found new direction. I chose restaurants that tickled my interest, ones that stood out as an original. I would spend a small amount of time in a lot of brilliant places. I left St John and went on a culinary pilgrimage. My motives were questionable but innocent. I needed to taste more victory. My next fix would be harder to come by, as I had to go bigger. This time I was looking for my own purpose.

FOO
PREC

DIS
IOUS

THE BEST CHEFS CAN'T COOK

MY CRUSADE TOOK ME
ALL OVER THE WORLD.

Instead of working at one restaurant per year, which is the norm, I went to dozens of different restaurants for a day, a week, a month – espresso shots of culinary worlds, sipping on perspective. I had complimentary glimpses into the minds of some brilliant chefs, soaking up many points of view.

The journey took me all the way to Australia, to a kitchen that was one of the world's best. At face value this place seemed exemplary — really unique food 'inspired by nature'. However, it was more of a factory. (A factory or a prison?) There were over 30 chefs working in this steamy dungeon. The different sections were run by different gangs, loaded with animosity and self-interest. Cooking in this kitchen was a world unto its own. Cutting flowers into 'natural' shapes with a scalpel, laying 'painted' carrot ribbons onto silicon with tweezers and organizing identical parsley stalks into test tubes. Welcome to the machine.

High standards mean pressure, long hours and an unhealthy appetite for competition. Perfection can be achieved by aligning all the variables precisely. This is enforced to achieve the best food in the world. It's a matter of many hands make light work. Program lots of chefs to do very little, perfectly. I was part of the protein gang; I had the duty of cooking the quail breasts. One day a senior chef decided he had a problem with me. He made it clear: my quail cooking technique was not how he wanted it. It was a routine 'show him who's boss', an exercise in flexing his authority. Although this guy was about as sharp as a spoon, a master of his own reality; his behaviour was befitting of the gang culture.

In a moment of bravery, I stepped away from the marching line and challenged him: I told him that he was wrong. He bellowed out a string of nonsensical sounds, like an angry ape. I replied, 'Let's both cook it in our own way and let the kitchen decide if mine is inferior.' His eyes began darting around as the remainder of his body became paralyzed in silence. Now speechless, he started pacing, chest out, fists clenched, eyes wide open. This gorilla knew he was wrong. He backed off, then ambled off into the steamy shadows. I continued cooking it my way.

You don't trust yourself as a young chef. You look up to these people who own million-pound restaurants, with titles and years of distinction, who have proven to be successful. I felt emboldened from challenging a leader, rebellion was growing within. There was another way forward.

One day, after a particularly gruesome shift, I stumbled outside and into the street. I was running low on life, worn out, losing faith, desperate for a way out. It was hot and raining heavily. I could hear music thudding in the distance. I gravitated in that direction until I saw a giant queue of people snaking around a mysterious building. I joined the queue as if it was a stairway to heaven. This profound monolith was like nothing I'd ever seen before. Like a moth to a flame, I followed the crowds inside.

The people swarmed around brightly coloured tables made from used tarpaulin. Giant kegs filling jam jars with beer. There were no windows, just huge gaps in the walls, bees buzzing through. Loquacious graffiti plastered everywhere, like prophetic inscriptions in a cave. The rich verdant garden on the roof grew from giant rusty barrels. The outer walls had thousands of little terracotta pots suspended in an old industrial frame carpeting the whole building, wild strawberries growing from each pot. The views were breathtaking, the music was loud, I was intoxicated. Good life existed here. I didn't know what was going on, but I had an intense feeling – this was my future.

The prestige bullshit I had just left behind was insignificant in the shadow of this holy temple. This was The Greenhouse by Joost (pronounced 'Yoast') Bakker, a man I would meet soon after, the Zero Waste prophet.

IMAGINE A WORLD WITHOUT WASTE

JOOST HAS A PRESENCE THAT I STRUGGLE TO DESCRIBE. IT IS AS IF HE IS FROM THE FUTURE.

Everything Joost said and did was so simple, his examples obvious, yet somehow nobody was doing them, which made his ideas so radical.

Joost talked about big subjects – how to innovate, how cities could grow food, how we are going to save the world. He would say things like, 'Imagine flying into a city and all you see is green.' He is a bonafide artist, a visionary and a man trying to make the world a better place. Without hesitation, I joined his posse of luminous disciples.

Joost had a business partner called Greg and one day I joined them both for lunch. They used big words that I didn't understand. I remember them throwing this one word around, this word I didn't know: 'sustainability'. I felt like I needed to engage them, finally, and so blurted out, 'What does sustainability mean?' There was a pause. They sat perplexed, probably thinking, 'Is he taking the piss or is this a deeply profound question?' These are brilliant men, but I don't think they had caught on to how absolutely clueless I was. I honestly had no idea what sustainability meant.

It's amazing how quickly you can learn a subject when your mind is open; moreover, when you're inspired by the same subject you're trying to understand – it's an intense download. I absorbed this world around me, I started to see something forming on the horizon.

Further down the line, Joost, myself and his army of disciples opened Silo by Joost, a little cafe in the centre of Melbourne. The plan was to use Silo as a testing space for the Greenhouse empire and as a place to attempt the virtuous idea of Zero Waste. Silo was born in Australia in 2014, written on the wall it read: Imagine a world without Waste.

Joost explained that to avoid packaging, we would make everything from scratch. Sounded pretty straightforward, then I realized – I would have to make sourdough bread. I had never made sourdough before. In order to make bread, I would have to mill flour, how the hell do you mill flour? I would have to learn how to make yoghurt, no idea. There would be pastry; I would need butter, which meant I would have to churn butter, to then mix with my fresh flour. We would need to make everything from scratch, with food straight from the farm.

I was working late one night, it was just me in the little cafe, I'd been drinking wine straight from the barrel. I was making shortbread when it hit me – not the wine, a revelation, one that would shape my professional life (and is why this book exists). I'd made fresh butter from this amazing fatty cream, and biodynamic flour had just come through our flour mill. I made the dough, which looked and felt very different to the shortbread I'd made hundreds of times before. Eventually, when this arduous biscuit came out of the oven, I tasted it. It blew my mind, 'How does this taste so good?' It was incredible.

This is the future of food, I thought. If this was what shortbread should taste like, what the hell is the shortbread that we've all been eating? I needed to tell the world of my findings. This was the beginning of a new thought process, right there and then. I had identified a pre-industrial food system (though I couldn't articulate this until much later):

Farmers are good, middlemen are not.
Middleman means processing and packaging;
Farmer means fresh, flavourful, fundamental food.

Getting things from nature in the way nature intended, food from the farm is real; food from the factory is not real. Real food tastes better.

Zero Waste had led to this unique position. Zero Waste is the future of food.

LIMITA
BRE
CREA

TION
EDS
TIVITY

WASTED

DO YOU EVER HAVE THE FEELING YOU'RE MORE ALIVE THAN NORMAL? ARE YOU LIVING IN THE PRESENT, NOT LOOKING TO THE PAST OR FUTURE?

It was at this time in Australia I had a daily belief that anything was possible. Silo was developing, Joost's empire was readying the campaign. We had this glorious proposition: a food system that generated Zero Waste. This was a very wholesome design, but I was curious to readjust my focus to ingredients considered to be 'waste'. I wanted to offer safe passage to those ingredients condemned without a fair trial, to demonstrate how everything has value, even if it wasn't immediately obvious. One man's waste is another man's treasure.

I created a pop-up dinner called WASTED. Ten courses of food that would have otherwise been wasted: nettles, animal fat, duck hearts, anchovy spines and herb stems were just some of the ingredients brought to the table. The idea was a noble one and I had lots of moral support. However, it was an initiative without the strength of a restaurant. Joost was busy starting an empire, I was on my own this time.

People have often called me 'brave', which I never really understand, as wouldn't I have to be scared to warrant 'bravery'? I'm now very aware that people confuse bravery with naivety. Imagine that eating magical jelly beans freed you of self-doubt. Being naive is like eating jelly beans without knowing their effect. When you eat the jelly beans you have a false sense of security, a rainbow-coloured force field protecting you, obscuring the view of danger. This confidence allows you to brave the unknown, march forward into new territory. However, when the jelly beans start to wear off, reality reveals itself. After the jelly beans are gone you think, 'Was I on drugs? How did I not consider the consequences?'

This pop-up was my first bite of reality, a consequence come-down, a blind leap of faith made possible by my own naivety. What seemed like a simple dinner became an anxious nightmare. Organizing a ten-course dinner in a foreign city, for over 100 guests, was way beyond me. I had only considered half of everything that needed to happen. Friends who helped me were spitting feathers – sleep deprived, confused and under unnecessary pressure. The first night of the pop-up was a car crash – all the ideas came out nothing like I'd imagined, the guests were very underwhelmed. We'd worked so hard only to disappoint. I felt that reality burn, it was awful. The shame got to me, so I obsessively put right all the wrongs, overnight.

The second night was the opposite. The jelly beans had worn off. We knuckled down, and all of a sudden the bright, shiny ideas made sense. There was a beautiful moment that night. It was late and we were five courses deep. I had just served a course titled 'Blood, brain and skin'. I'd poached the brains into small nuggets coated with crispy pork crackling. The blood was cooked with spices similar in nature to a black pudding, blended into a thick paste coating the crispy brains. This was the course I assumed people would find too challenging, but joy of joys, the plates were returned to the kitchen…CLEAN. They loved it!

After hours of chaos, I'd caught my tail. The energy in the room was electric, questioning 'What just happened?' The guests appeared to be shocked by the meal, yet the concept felt quite unremarkable to me. It was just rational thought: make waste delicious.

I sometimes look back at how naive I was in those days, cringing at the madness. However, that naivety was a blessing in disguise. The WASTED dinners wouldn't have happened if I had realistic doubts in my mind. It's important to note that this impetuous behaviour needs a counterbalance, a commitment to follow through and clean up after yourself. Be willing to fail and don't get cocky when you taste victory. Creativity is simply connecting dots, putting information together in a unique way. Self-doubt will sabotage creativity. God bless the jelly beans.

THE VEGANS ARE COMING

WHILE I WAS WORKING FOR JOOST, I WAS CAPTIVATED BY MANY THINGS, BUT VEGANISM WAS NOT ONE OF THEM.

However, the future of food was an oasis in my mind. I saw rich, verdant pastures, complex interconnected life, plants on plants. It was a mere mirage at this point. Nonetheless, this mirage had my attention. The future of food is mostly about plants.

My Australian fairytale came to its natural end, England had beckoned me back. It was an obligation. I was back home, where there were no farmers' markets, no organic farms – food is considered fuel. Vegan seemed the only rational path – buying animal products would be a subversion. The only thing I could justify was plant-based. This was an opportunity to get ahead, broaden my vision, prepare for the coming vegan horde. Learning to cook without meat or dairy is like learning how to speak French: you can easily learn a few words, but if you want to do it well you have to change the way you think, you have to commit.

The vegan cults of the day had one major agenda: no animal products. The priority was never deliciousness, rarely about local farming and certainly not about innovation. I was cooking vegan food day and night, some good, some bad, mostly just OK. Occasionally I'd see something glimmer, a diamond in the rough. Vegan food is typically made up of dozens of ingredients together; I insisted on just a few main ingredients. Cooking dozens of ingredients spreads your attention too thin and gives little respect to the precious vegetable. But how can just three plant-based ingredients make your palette bliss out?

The new approach was emerging. I was observing vegetables through a magnifying glass. Through the process of elimination, I would uncover their secrets, like being a detective, a vegetable detective. They were all suspects. I interrogated countless vegetables, steaming them, provoking them, making them sweat. Eventually one of them would talk. I'd follow that lead and often find a clue. When most chefs interrogate a vegetable, they don't look close enough, they just ask the basic questions and let the vegetables move on, rarely finding something original. If you understand why they're sweating, you know there's something going on. Savvy interrogation reveals new potential. God is in the details.

One crucial piece of evidence that I found (and still embrace today) is to create a solid foundation of texture within a vegetable, ideally a larger vegetable with a neutral flavour. This is best achieved by multi-stage cooking/drying/hydrating, to create a complex meaty texture. This structure forms a base that can then be applied liberally with flavours and other magical elements. This creates a central unified theme of togetherness from which people subconsciously gain primal satisfaction – a similar satisfaction as one gets from eating a steak.

One day I decided to cook a whole pumpkin. It began with steam, opening its pores to ready it for caramelization. I then found the sweet-spot dry-roasting temperature, summoning the sweet juices to surface, slowly turning to caramel. Then it was chilled in the fridge, sliced into an appropriate portion and dried for hours, concentrating the large, leathery orange chunk. I felt confident, I was going for the kill. I soaked the 'steak' until its body was supple, before blasting it once again with high heat, letting its head blister and its skin sear. The pumpkin lay defeated, the perfect kill. I finished it off with a sauce of toasted pumpkin seeds and sorrel lathered over the steamy orange corpse.

A divine moment, this vegetable had gone beyond the pale. Something new lay before me. It wasn't a masterpiece, only the map revealing where to find one. The rise of veganism is extraordinary. Regardless of where my values differ, vegans are a big part of the future and a big part of Silo's future. We will champion a new wave of vegan food, but do it our own way – with quality as a priority. An opulent plate of plants, perhaps even a masterpiece.

PROG
I
ME

RESS
S
SSY

THE DARK DAYS

WHETHER BY THE GRACE OF A GODDESS, A DARK LORD, OR ANOTHER SERENDIPITOUS FORCE, I ENDED UP WANDERING THE STREETS OF BRIGHTON ON A GREY RAINY DAY IN JANUARY.

I had strayed far from my path. I was walking down a residential street when I saw a huge old warehouse, weathered, with lots of character. There was an old-school 6-metre (20-ft) rolling door. I saw huge wooden beams through the big window, a high ceiling and white flint walls. The building was being used as storage, no 'for sale' signs. I knew immediately that this would be the birthplace of Silo.

Several potential partners had all bought into my vision, but when it came to money and bank transfers they turned the other way. They didn't take my vegetable steak seriously. At what seemed to be the bitter end, after a year of efforts, a guardian angel of sorts revealed the answer: remortgage your house. This paltry investment meant that I would have to get very creative. That was the beginning of Silo.

Some weeks before Silo became official, the biggest newspaper in the UK somehow got wind of my intentions. Within the space of 24 hours, the article went live with the simple title, 'First zero-waste restaurant opens in Brighton'. It went viral before Silo was even official. I advise everyone to never read comments about yourself online, it's not healthy. I didn't have this advice and it nearly broke my spirit before I'd started. One particular comment stood out. It stated, simply: 'Silo will fail.' The commenter looked at the Silo model and criticized it for being utopic, that it could not survive, that we were a nanoscale production which could not compete with today's industrial efficiency. It was thoughtful and well articulated. The only thing I could think was 'I can't let Silo fail.'

The early days of Silo were very dark; literal darkness. There were services where there was no electricity, days when the basement would flood. Chefs were ankle-deep in the water working on benches lit from the torches of their phones. The reality was tough, chaotic and intense. Staff were dropping like flies. How had life descended to this?

I would be scrubbing jam jars at 3am, sleeping on the restaurant floor – there were weeks where I didn't leave the building. I became everybody's worst nightmare. I was angry, scatty and an awful leader. This manic behaviour led to many burnt bridges. The restaurant manager once sent out a group email saying I needed psychological help. I insisted on Zero Waste relentlessly, to the point where we used a coconut instead of a scouring pad. I probably did need help. One day the building nearly burnt down because my chefs would sneak oily cloths into the washing machine. The machine combusted into flames, the customers evacuated their lunches as we called the fire brigade. I was in a dark place, but I kept moving towards the light. What else do you do when you're lost and desperate? You keep going!

Silo is a statement – at the time, an untested statement. We were trying to implement an idea in a place where it was not welcome. There weren't any instructions, there was no map. Silo's life was a perilous voyage, with frequent casualties. I've burnt so many people along the way and it didn't feel good. The important detail I haven't mentioned, however, is that we were really busy. About six months in, after countless gruesome battles, there was a particularly memorable Saturday. The restaurant was packed with zombies pushing to eat, the queue outside was swelling, the music was fierce and victory was in the air. The restaurant manager turned to me and said, 'We've created a monster.'

Those days were undoubtedly dark, but the crawl towards the light wasn't for nothing. We were winning national awards and being constantly bombarded by the press, and the relentless zombie hordes just kept coming. When I wasn't disintegrating on life support, I was drunk on success.

'I DON'T DO DRUGS, I AM DRUGS'

I'D LIKE TO TAKE YOU THROUGH A ZERO WASTE WORMHOLE: TAKE A LOOK THROUGH MY SILO-DESCOPE.

Not having a bin meant going directly to farmers, and buying from farmers isn't easy. They're often late, they don't want to change their routine, their communication leaves a lot to be desired, you see 20 products on their list (if they have a list), then when you see the farm you realize they have 60 products and some more appealing than the products on the list, such as vegetables with mad, inconsistent shapes.

When you get cream from the cow it's never the same twice, so how do you then follow a recipe? When you churn butter and have an abundance of uncultured buttermilk, what do you do with it? Cheese gives you whey, lots. When you mill flour it's not fine, so how do you sift the flour? Every question resulted in more questions. These questions were put through our priority filter, which resulted in action. This action led to lots of failures, but every now and again a success. This was usually the order: failure, failure, failure, failure, kind of success, failure, failure, failure, success.

Various failures included:
- We made our own soap, but it cost us too much time.
- We tried to grow mushrooms, but it required too much attention.
- I tried to pick up all the products myself in a van, but me leaving Silo was calamitous.
- We tried to integrate front-of-house (FOH) and the kitchen, but chefs were afraid of customers and FOH afraid of long hours.
- We tried to serve raw milk but someone said they nearly died.

For every ten things we tried, maybe one would succeed. When you own a commercial business, it's not ideal to work at 10% efficiency.

I sometimes wonder what cosmic force has held Silo together. When I think back to all the mistakes, I start to understand how people find religion: our survival was unexplainable. Restaurants run smoothly when there is consistency; Silo was about as consistent as the Wild West. We didn't know what would survive, a lot of ideas died horribly, thankfully some survivors lived to tell the tale. There's an agricultural idea called a landrace. A farmer throws down 100 different varieties of seed into his field. A year later he has witnessed the strongest outmuscle the weak. The farmer can then grow the strongest seeds, having confidence and foresight. A landrace is a pragmatic approach not unusual to farmers. However, such an approach in hospitality would be considered abnormal. Silo was a landrace. We were throwing down hundreds of seeds to understand the relationship between a Zero Waste system and a commercial restaurant.

When I look back over that time, I can appreciate how important it was. On my knees, I prayed to the gods of Zero Waste for their protection. It wasn't as romantic as it sounds, but the struggle bore fruit, and I now have the answers, thanks to all those mistakes. Mistakes are precious, I deplore the shame, it's the best way to learn. They keep you humble, keep you sharp and keep things interesting. The early years were a bubbling fermentation tank of creativity, living on adrenaline and wild ideas. As Salvador Dali put it: 'I DON'T DO DRUGS, I AM DRUGS.'

It took a long time before the formula started to reveal itself. Before then I was just spinning through the fog with no rules. Now the rules are clear, rules I can swear by. The fog has cleared. I've always wanted Silo to be an example, charting a course, ethically, sustainably, morally. Like an infant, we grew so quickly, falling down and getting up again. Smiling one moment then crying the next. I want to create change. I have a lot to prove and I knew I was digging in the right place, but this wasn't a dig for fame and fortune.

To me, this is the blueprint for the future.

EVERY
|
CONN

THING
S
ECTED

CARROTS COOKED IN COMPOST

ONE NIGHT, AFTER EVERYONE HAD GONE HOME, DELIRIOUS AND EXHAUSTED I FOUND MYSELF STARING INTO THE COMPOST MACHINE.

I picked up a handful of the spongy brown compost – it smelt like a Christmas pudding, and lemon. I thought it was odd, that it could smell so citrusy. We don't even use lemons.

I discovered later that the brewers who make our botanical drinks had deposited 60 kilograms (132lb) of lemon waste into our compost machine a few days prior. They had intercepted the lemons before they would have been dumped into landfill. The lemons were considered unfit for the supermarket, based on an aesthetically imperfect form.

As I sat in there deep in thought, I happened to have a crate of carrots next to me. Maybe it was the sleep deprivation, maybe it was a cosmic serendipitous force, but it seemed only rational to cook the carrots in the compost. I made a dough out of the compost with 2% salt and wrapped the carrots in the citrusy brown dough. I baked them, and do you know what? They tasted of lemon. The right kind of lemon – fragrant, bright, zesty but not acidic. The colour was a deep, dark orange, the texture was like fudge and they were oh-so sweet. The best carrots I had ever eaten.

The incredible transfer of flavour was profound. It just looked like compost, but the flavour was so clean. Considering the compost is like a graveyard for food waste, I kept thinking of this lemony presence as reincarnation. The lemons' essence had been reborn in my carrots. When I ate the carrots, it was as like taking part in a lemony seance, communicating with the citrus spirit.

Being creative means that I was open to an idea. If I wasn't open, I would not have followed this though; I probably wouldn't have connected the dots and just gone home to bed. Being open is allowing yourself to wander into the unknown, seeing new things as an opportunity, then simply acting upon that opportunity.

A small while after my profound carrot moment, I got an invite from my food hero and one of the best chefs in the world, Dan Barber. I first discovered Dan when I watched his TED Talk, around the time I'd moved to Oz. It was a very intelligent talk about how to feed the world, executed poetically with lots of humour. I became mildly obsessed with this talk. I knew all the words and I'd find myself quoting Dan when in the throes of a passionate debate. Dan Barber was the third Silo influencer, after James and Joost.

I was to be a guest chef at his dinner concept called WASTED, a prestigious dinner on the rooftop of Selfridge's in central London, championing food that would have otherwise gone to waste. I couldn't believe that Dan Barber had the exact same idea as I did, it was flattering and simultaneously a freak coincidence. When I spoke to him about it, there was no doubt – he genuinely had no idea that I had also done a Wasted pop-up dinner.

A week before the dinner we strategically remastered the compost formula, daily drip-feeding buckets of lemony waste. The day of the event, I decided that we would smoke the carrots after cooking them – an impulsive decision that could have ended in disaster. My sous chef was in charge of smoking the carrots, which he did in a separate prep kitchen. He would scurry through, giving me a slither of carrot to test its level of smoke. I kept saying 'more', over and over. He told me the extraction fan wasn't working and that the kitchen was filled with black smoke. 'More!' I said, like a madman, as his face turned a pale white. Eventually, we got it right, just before he fainted and we nearly burnt down one of London's largest buildings.

As the smoke cleared, I knew we had ourselves a remarkable product. We served them with curds and whey. It was a bold dish that drove the Silo flag deep into the ground. Dan Barber's response to eating the dish was simple: 'Astonishing'.

EXISTENTIAL ICE CREAM

SILO WAS AWARDED THE DISTINCTION OF BEING 'BRITAIN'S MOST ETHICAL RESTAURANT'. THIS WAS A GREAT SUCCESS.

It was an award voted for by the people. Being ethical isn't easy, or at least trying to understand what's most ethical with indecent circumstances. I have had numerous staff resent me and my so-called 'ethicalism'.

I'm the first to admit that my leadership has been bullish, working people extremely hard and not paying them as much as I'd like to. However, there's something I've known for many years, but been unable to articulate until now. The reality of being ethical is championing ethical activities to the limit of what you can sustain. There's a reason why hospitality is poorly paid, there's a reason why cheap food exists, there's a reason why animals suffer for our greed – the world is far from perfect.

Silo and its ethical banner fly high, attracting all things 'ethical'. This is a wonderful thing. However, we're still human, an imperfect mass of cells. The reality is a compromise – however, compromising in the right places – in a fight to sustain the mission. The goal of Silo is to demonstrate a natural food system of the future, with Zero Waste as its USP. This means doing things properly. Doing things properly means high labour costs, and where does that money come from? Maybe upping prices to balance it out? I've found that the more you tinker with the system, the more you get electrocuted. For every action, there is an equal or opposite reaction.

Ice cream is not ethical, although everyone loves it – creamy, luxuriously good times. Another perspective reveals a sinister reality, a complex underground labyrinth against a droning hum of machinery, cow juice and chicken ovary mix industrially wed into an unholy matrimony – an endless siphon of cattle and poultry excrement to supply frozen maniacal pleasure.

The more you look at nature, the more industrial products seem absurd. If we all agree that industrial farming is a sin, then we must consider the reality of making ice cream from non-industrial produce. Cows roaming on grass, chickens ambling through the hedgerows, all giving their natural bounty when it's in season. This would result in no ice cream for most of the year and when we could buy the ice cream it would cost more than caviar. Could you even imagine?

Human innovation brought us domesticity of cows and chickens, and, subsequently, ice cream. At Silo, we are creating natural food in an industrial world and trying to innovate with what is available. That said, a chicken's egg and cow juice, two animal components to make one dish, is a step too far.

Things are weirder than we think. And these weird moments can be liberating. Life is older, richer in possibilities, things don't have to be the way they are. At one point it might have seemed wildly innovative to take a chicken ovary with cow's breast milk and put those two together to form a dessert. This mutant combination birthed something delicious. With that same thinking, out of Silo's lab: a potato ice cream that has no chicken eggs and cow juice. Made from the roasted skins of waxy potatoes, it tastes similar to salted caramel. Complemented with stunning blackcurrants, big fat jammy little orbs, and fennel flowers bursting with spiced deliciousness.

Revelations happen when you break a pattern of thought. In a parallel universe, our cattle overlords are looking in on an industrial snowglobe. They can see outside the bubble. Dairy is debatably natural, what other animals drink another animal's breast milk? However, what if that animal is raised sustainably, for the purpose of agricultural prosperity? Perhaps I'm just justifying dairy's deliciousness for my own selfish culinary pursuits.

Cross-hybridization of animal excrement doesn't feel right. The pursuit of happiness through ice cream can be a purpose. But there's a line, a balance of reality. With dairy, if it's a happy animal processed naturally for the benefit of agriculture, I will proudly serve it.

2

IDEAS

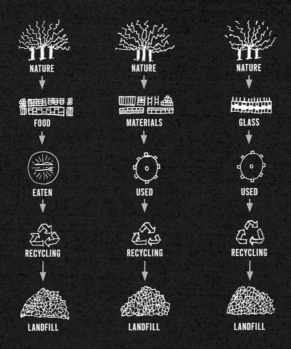

NATURE   NATURE   NATURE

FOOD   MATERIALS   GLASS

EATEN   USED   USED

RECYCLING   RECYCLING   RECYCLING

LANDFILL   LANDFILL   LANDFILL

AN INDUSTRIAL FOOD SYSTEM

It's important to note that industrialism is brilliant: it's the reason for human prosperity. Of course it's not a perfect system and it's crucial we see it for all its flaws. Recycling is an industrial process built to tackle waste, yet it itself creates various forms of waste: material, time, energy, space, money.

Unfortunately, recycling is industrialism's best-case scenario. At the point of writing this book, the global waste/landfill statistics are: 30% of food goes to landfill, 80% of plastic goes to landfill (or is incinerated) and nearly 40% of glass goes to landfill. This highlights only the three primary materials of an industrial food system, just enough to make the point.

NATURE	NATURE	NATURE
FOOD	NATURAL MATERIALS	GLASS
EATEN	USED	USED
GREEN COMPOST	BROWN COMPOST	GLASS POWDER
NATURE	NATURE	WORKSHOP

A SILO FOOD SYSTEM

The true aim of Zero Waste is to work only with natural materials, letting everything live its life then return to nature. Being part of an industrial world, full of non-natural materials, this is nearly impossible. The next achievable goal is to 'not recycle', taking ownership for every material that enters your system. Choose materials that live productive, long lives, that can be reborn into something new. The term for this process is 'cradle to cradle'.

Recycling is to turn something back into the same thing. Cradle to cradle is to turn something into a new thing, ideally a better thing that can then feed back into the system. For example, crushing single-use glass into powder, which then gets made directly into things that are needed, such as plates, cups and tiles. This is a closed-loop circular system, cradle to cradle, nature to nature.

ZERO WASTE: FOOD

THE FIRST AND MOST IMPORTANT MATERIAL IS FOOD. ALL OUR FOOD COMES DIRECTLY FROM THE FARMS, THE SEA, THE WILD, THE BOATS AND THE DAIRY.

We get our ingredients directly from nature, so the food is whole. This is ideal as it means we avoid unnecessary packaging. Furthermore, it means we can process at will, allowing us to control the quality and freshness – and the by-products. Industrialization processes whole food for us, meaning we don't see the by-products. A lot of them are wasted, or used in a way which is not natural.

We aim to put as much as possible on the plate: to maximize resources is to minimize waste. With imagination, experience and commitment we can turn every scrap into something special: there's no such thing as a by-product, just another product.

There is some inevitable food that doesn't get consumed, such as egg shells, customers' plate waste and our 'mistakes' – this all gets composted and used to grow food.

IT'S A CLOSED LOOP.

NATURE

FOOD

EATEN

GREEN COMPOST

NATURE

ZERO WASTE: NATURAL MATERIALS

THE SECOND CATEGORY IS MATERIAL WASTE, BOTH NATURAL AND INDUSTRIAL.

Cardboard, paper and napkins come from industrial productions. This is where industrial efficiency is very effective, especially if the production is ecologically positive. It would be delusional to think that all our materials were created from endlessly renewable material sources and powered by green energy.

Zero Waste is at its best when trading in reusable vessels. When that's not possible, for example, getting napkins from a courier, the small amount of excess paper/cardboard packaging that is used can then be composted.

This is how ingredients can be delivered:

- Fruit and vegetables in crates.
- Dry ingredients, such as wheat, oats, seeds, in bulk paper bags.
- Milk and cream in stainless steel pails and/or large jerry cans that can be endlessly reused.
- Wild food gathered in tote bags/baskets.
- Fish in reusable containers.
- Meat bought in whole animal form, or halves/quarters, then butchered and smothered in rendered fat.
- Coffee and tea in an airtight container.
- Chocolate in big slabs wrapped in brown paper.
- Botanical drinks, such as kombucha, kefir and ale, in Cornelius kegs.
- Some special couriers can be used – insist on biodegradable packaging, including latex adhesive tape.
- Wine in glass bottles (see next page).

All of the used natural packaging gets composted and used to grow food.

IT'S A CLOSED LOOP.

NATURE

NATURAL MATERIALS

USED

BROWN COMPOST

NATURE

ZERO WASTE: GLASS

THE THIRD PRIMARY MATERIAL WE USE IS GLASS.

This was our dilemma:

- England doesn't produce natural wine, with only a couple of exceptions.
- Wine from France (and further afield) doesn't have an infrastructure to accommodate reusable kegs.
- If we want natural wine, we have to accept single-use glass.

For years we recycled our single-use glass. Our Zero Waste motive is 'to not recycle'. After a great deal of research we discovered a way of upcycling our glass into a new material that has value to the restaurant. We turn our waste glass into sand, then into powder, then into a stable emulsion, allowing us to cast it into a new material. We call it 'glass porcelain'.

This new material has so much potential – the ecological implications for the process are staggering, especially when you consider it on an industrial scale. The glass powder gets melted at temperatures over 1,000 degrees lower than glass recycling, with minimal energy used, crushing from bottle to powder. Economically, this process is extremely compelling, especially considering the small investment to set up. We're turning waste that costs nothing into something precious that we need, like a plate.

Creatively speaking, this process has endless opportunities, from making bathroom tiles or paper-thin teacups, to choosing the colour of a wine bottle or influencing it with various oxides and painting or glazing it. We have only scratched the surface. Most importantly, this process means that we can avoid recycling and take control of our system, preventing waste and creating the things we need.

IT'S A CLOSED LOOP.

NATURE

GLASS

USED

GLASS POWDER

WORKSHOP

THE SILO DIET

SILO IS VERY PRO-VEGAN AND PALEO. THESE TWO TRIBES HAVE GREAT REASONS TO EAT AS THEY DO, THE KEY TOPICS BEING ETHICS, HEALTH AND SUSTAINABILITY.

The Silo diet as a title would be 'Pre-industrial'. As detailed throughout this book, we believe the big problem is industrialism. The world gets more ill as the food system becomes more industrial.

INDUSTRIALISM:

Ethics Industrial food systems force nature to do what benefits humans. From the perspective of all the other species, this is selfish and unethical.

Sustainability In a very short space of time, industrialism has damaged the ozone layer, polluted the oceans and degraded the fertility of the planet. This is, of course, unsustainable.

Health Industrialism has given humans longer lives through advanced medicine. However, it is making us very ill during these long lives, namely due to processed and chemically engineered food, and by providing the diet that we want – not what we need.

It's valuable to draw comparison to the most popular alternative diets with similar motivations – vegan and paleo. Where we differ from vegan: we believe that all the meat and dairy we serve is ethical, sustainable and natural. Where we differ from paleo: we have different thoughts on the definition of 'natural'. We believe that agriculture is less natural than wild food. However, agriculture is now a part of nature; furthermore, it's the only way to feed the world.

	VEGAN	PALEO	SILO
MEAT	NO	YES	YES
DAIRY	NO	NO	YES
GRAINS	YES	NO	YES
FRUIT	YES	YES	YES
VEG	YES	YES	YES
WILD	YES	LOTS	YES
FISH	NO	YES	YES
Priorities	*Nothing animal*	*Pre-agriculture*	*Pro-agriculture*

A NOTE ON FERMENTED FOOD Whether vegan or paleo, there's one principle we can all agree on: fermented food. Fermentation is one of the most pre-industrial food technologies we know of – an ancient form of preservation that is literally pre-history. While we don't really understand where and when this way of working with food began, harnessing the unseen world of bacteria will bring us physiological well-being, namely to our guts.

A natural (Silo) diet is fundamentally interconnected with and interdependent on our environment. Humans are what we call 'holobionts' – vast ecologies comprising both human cells and trillions of microbes. Industrial food threatens the biodiversity of our microbiome (the micro-organisms in a particular environment). Fermenting food into gut-friendly superfoods is an antidote to this processed industrial food.

CAN EATING MEAT BE ETHICAL?

HAVE YOU EVER GOT INTO A DEBATE WITH AN ANIMAL RIGHTS ACTIVIST ABOUT MEAT CONSUMPTION?

There's a good chance you didn't win the argument. There are very few ways to justify eating meat. The reality is that the majority of meat that's eaten is unethical. It boils down to the simple fact that the *unnecessary* death of an animal cannot be justified. This is the cow-shaped elephant in the room.

However, there are a few examples where the death of an animal *is* necessary, namely the creature's invasive nature; an external species outcompeting the native species of the said ecosystem. A deer without its natural predator can damage an environment; ethically speaking, we can play wolf. Rabbits are another pest – from a naturalist's perspective it's necessary that they die. This then gets into philosophical territory, and maybe we don't have the right to play god.

Likewise with fish. There are a number of examples where there is an unnatural balance, be it crayfish invading our rivers or cephalopods (squid, octopus) overpopulating our oceans.

While our evolution suggests we humans are frugivores, we clearly have the ability to eat meat, and have done so for tens of thousands of years. The most sustainable agriculture *is* inclusive of animals; however, it doesn't necessarily mean we should kill the animal. If our agricultural systems benefit from the inclusion of animals, can we ethically take their milk? More on this later.

Silo has always served meat – this has been a point of contention from the beginning.

Firstly – it's been our mission to create positive change. Fundamentally, meat is part of that system of change.
Secondly – the meat we serve would have gone to waste, regardless of our intervention.
Lastly – it comes from organic places, be it a farm or the wild.

Examples of ethical meat and fish:

- Invasive animals
- Retired breeding animals, dairy cows and dairy veal calves that would have otherwise been wasted
- Roadkill
- Lab meat
- Creatures that are overpopulated through 'cracks' in biodiversity
- Fish that don't have a brain or nervous system*

*Eating a creature that has no face, no brain and no nervous system (invertebrates) is ethically no different to eating a vegetable. Furthermore, there are positives to eating certain creatures – oysters, for example, purify the surrounding water, so eating those delicious creatures (farmed/caught responsibly) is ecologically positive, or 'bio-benign'.

A NOTE ON DAIRY The largest motivation separating vegan from vegetarian is the unethical reality of the dairy industry. However, we passionately believe that the problem isn't dairy per se; rather, it's the way in which the dairy industry is managed. Raising millions of cows in metal sheds against their will, pumped full of hormones, and slaughtering veal calves and taking what we want is odious and repugnant, a disgrace to nature.

However, there are many examples, mostly pre-industrial, that are ethical – animals living symbiotically with humans. The consumption of dairy is itself a point of ethics. As described in 'Existential Ice Cream' (see pages 44–45) it's a precious, delicious food source that should be eaten respectfully, not as a commodity.

DIRECT TRADE VS INDIRECT TRADE

Direct trade is the most important part of a Zero Waste system. When you trade with nature there's no packaging. Industrialism has created indirect trade, which means division between origin and consumer. This is why so much waste exists in the food system. This division is managed by centralized government and large corporations. They are held accountable for our safety. Unfortunately they overcompensate, turning food that's alive into food that's not alive, which basically means they kill all bacteria. No bacteria means that we don't get sick – in the short term. In the long term, eating this processed dead food makes us very ill.

For further safety and convenience, the industrial system wraps our food in packaging, creating more waste.

The other big problem with this indirect trade is guessing what the consumer wants and how much of it they want. This guesswork massively overcompensates, creating industrial quantities of waste food.

Lastly, and perhaps most importantly, when we are, as consumers, detached from nature, our food culture changes, making us apathetic. The long-term effects are profound.

DIRECT TRADE
Pros – generates respect; the food is 'more alive', little/no waste, transparency, greater quality, better economical margins on both sides, more organic growth.
Cons – expensive for the supplier to manage trade, inconvenient for the chef by limiting delivery times and choice, not aligned with way most kitchens are operated today.

DIRECT TRADE

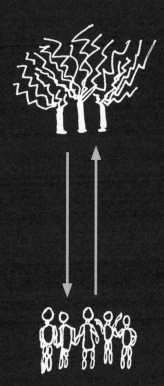

INDIRECT TRADE

INDIRECT TRADE
Pros – wholesale convenience and choice, price and delivery flexibility, control of distribution, reliability.
Cons – not transparent, inconsistent quality due to holding stock, more money to the middleman means less money for the chef and farmer, generates apathy, dead food, excessive waste, environmental damage. The bigger the scale, the worse for all the above.

THE FUTURE OF DIRECT TRADE – A DECENTRALIZED TECHNOLOGICAL NETWORK

The industrial food system is largely reliant on 'the middleman'. The middleman buys food from the farmer, processes it, packages it, holds it in convenient locations and then distributes it to the consumer. As previously mentioned, this is why waste exists, and this is why the natural integrity of food is lost.

In the future, this middleman will lose his job(s) to technology; direct trade operating on a decentralized platform, using the network to its own advantage, with partners sharing in the growth of the network. Technology can reconnect the farmer with the consumer. We will be able to trade directly with farms, allowing food to come into our kitchens 'alive', avoiding unnecessary packaging and activating accurate quantities of the product for the consumer.

DECENTRALIZED TECHNOLOGICAL NETWORK
Pros – producers get access to market, leveraging distribution strength of the network; this benefits direct trade, with 100% transparency due to shared network; incentivizes good behaviour and collaboration; leverages automated shared economy for communication (ordering) and transport, leading to services at marginal cost; wholesale makes 30%, whereas the network can be 15% or less, shared between farmers and chefs. Cons – puts the middleman out of a job as they know it; disruption to the food industry.

THE FUTURE OF DIRECT TRADE

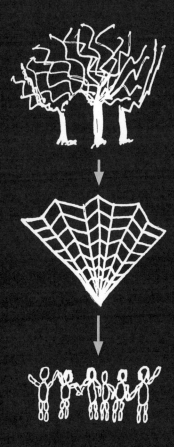

A NOTE ON TRANSPARENCY By being connected to the farmers and producers, not just as individuals but as communities, we can reconnect people to 'the nature of food'. Paired with a collaborative approach, this can create enough efficiencies to make higher quality food more accessible, lowering the cost.

WHY CAN WE STOMACH SPENDING BIG MONEY ON GOOD WINE BUT NOT ON GOOD TEA?

All the communities around the world reliant on tea are squashed by commodity pricing; controlled by 'Big Tea', sold to an unconcerned customer. The stakes are high: to change the public's perception before the artisan producers disappear.

Problems

- Lack of knowledge and appreciation for the value of a carefully crafted and delicious leaf above industrial product.

- No relationship between buyer/consumer and farmer – it all goes through faceless brokers and commodity auctions.

- Industrial processing for volume and price is the accepted norm.

- We cling to the old bag without questioning why.

- We cling to symbols and big brands.

- Tea companies, even some of the small, cool-looking ones, are typically owned by vast agri-businesses and multinational corporations, where profit wins over ethics.

ZERO WASTE We receive both tea and coffee i

We're emotionally attached to cheap bags of branded tea – as if good tea is an affectation, a betrayal of some kind. But what about their brothers and sisters in India and Africa, getting it in the neck for that cheap bag? Shouldn't our emotion be behind their plight, and rushing to help them?

Direct trade is the crucial step to avoid the industrial machine and move away from the processed product of large agri-businesses. Real relationships, both with farms and customers, are essential.

A cup of tea from a carefully chosen range, crafted by skilled men and women on independent farms, bought direct from farmers – not as a commodity from brokers – is well worth savouring.

Solutions

- Compare hand-crafted tea leaves with an industrial bag. Drink them side by side. You'll never go back.

- Prefer independent, direct-trade tea companies who know and support their farmers.

- Choose a beautiful leaf crafted for taste rather than cost.

- Embrace new tea: open your mind, your arms and your teapot.

- Find out where it comes from, who made it and how.

- By supporting direct trade and responsible relationships, we might force big business to change the way it works with producers, from exploitation to partnership.

special airtight containers.

COFFEE

WHERE DOES YOUR COFFEE COME FROM? CHEAP COFFEE FROM DUBIOUS ORIGINS HAS BECOME THE NORM, BUT THIS CAN CHANGE.

Coffee is processed in different ways, namely 'washed' and 'natural'. Washing coffee beans uses a phenomenal quantity of fresh water, often in hot countries with water limitations.

Problems

- The equitable nature of coffee is largely disparitive; coffee producers often live in abject poverty.

- Buying cheap coffee from large chains is unsustainable.

- Packaging and single-serve pods, which are not recyclable worldwide, create a huge level of waste.

- Paper cups have created such a problem that there is now a 'latte levy' in London to offset the cost of having to dispose of so many non-reusable items that find their way into the bins.

- Massive carbon footprint of shipping coffee worldwide.

ZERO WASTE We receive both tea and coffee i

As with raw milk, there are various safety, quality-control issues with natural coffee. Fundamentally, though, it's far more ecological to choose natural, and its consistency issues can result in expressive flavours.

As coffee doesn't grow in Europe, the carbon footprint provides a tough challenge. If you can access information about the coffee – origin, region, farm, grower, processing, variety, altitude and crop year – it's a good indication that the coffee has traceability and has been ethically sourced.

No one can stem the coffee-culture tide, but if you buy your coffee in reusable packaging and compost your used grinds, you're partway there to making it ethical.

Solutions

- Marginally raise the value of coffee. Buying from independently owned and operated companies within local communities allows them to have greater purchasing power in buying traceable coffee.

- Purchase coffee from your local cafe, even better if they roast their own.

- By using a cafetiere, stove top, pourover or other manual brewing device you are closing that gap in the waste system.

- Cafes offer a discount for bringing your own reusable cup.

- Purchase coffee from companies that are interested/committed to carbon neutrality.

special airtight containers.

BOTANICAL DRINKS

BREWING BOTANICAL DRINKS BENEFITS PLANET AND PEOPLE.

The natural world abounds with solutions to all our problems. Botanical drinks are made with live cultures and provide a much healthier, natural alternative to mass-produced drinks.

Problems

- Entrenched and addictive drink habits.

- Harmful stimulants packed into the products of powerful drink brands.

- Loss of biodiversity that comes from creating the vast monocultures needed to supply the drinks industry.

- Dependence on fossil fuels for cheap drinks.

- Heavy use of pesticides and fertilizers.

- Nutrient-less, synthetic ingredients.

ZERO WASTE We receive all the drinks in kegs;

The Old Tree Brewery – a brewery that operates like an old tree – is the craft drink maker of Silo, combining brewing and gardening to make nourishing drinks. Plants and microbes are harnessed for good in cultivated 'drinks forests', in which all the organic nutrients are composted. Food-forestry and fermentation are combined for health and earth repair, making a world in which we can eat and drink our own gardens – and our gardens are everywhere.

This ecological world provides a rich habitat for many creatures, as well as startlingly fresh drinks that change colour with the seasons.

Solutions

- Small, local breweries can regenerate the earth through urban composting.

- Seasonal ingredients increase long-term productivity while protecting the soil.

- A new fermentation culture will preserve traditions and empower plant knowledge.

- Harness the power of plants and natural microbes for health.

- Build community and create desirable outdoor work.

small batches in barrels with little taps.

WINE

COMMANDEERED BY BIG BUSINESS, THE WINE INDUSTRY HAS BECOME FAR REMOVED FROM ITS NATURAL ORIGINS.

Conventional wine has become a chemical process due to big corporations providing more at a lower cost. We know this is not sustainable.

Problems

- Blind acceptance of conventional wine, despite its destruction of our ecosystem and health.

- The way most wine is made is harmful to the planet, the winemakers and the consumers.

- Natural wine is still considered a gimmick.

- Misconception that natural wine tastes different to conventional wine.

- Natural wine can cost more, as any crafted/small-scale product should. Industrially produced wine has set false prices and assumptions of quality.

ZERO WASTE We turn our wine bottles into the

The farmer works without pesticides on the vineyard, which requires more attention, work and dependence on the weather. In the cellar, the farmer becomes winemaker and assists the wine, rather than controlling it with chemical, enzymes and technological methods.

Wine plays a vital part in the culinary world. It can make a dish sing, it can create an amazing balance of flavours, it can add kick to more subtle flavours. Wines filled with life and character will uplift the taste of natural ingredients and complement flavour combinations. The first bite of a dish and sip of the matching wine creates a harmony. It is a beautiful moment, which brings a lot of pleasure and joy.

Solutions

- Transparent labels, including information about the chemicals, pesticides and manipulation used.

- Better public knowledge about the person behind the wine, rather than the brand.

- Share knowledge and understanding of natural wine and what is behind the different legislations: organic, biodynamic, natural.

- Relearn the tastes of real wine, seeing commercial wine as we see processed food.

- The catering industry can take the lead and provide only 'crafted' natural wine. If we accept to pay more for organic food, we must do the same with our drinks.

things that we 'need', like plates and tiles.

WHY ISN'T IT COMMON FOR COCKTAILS TO BE PAIRED WITH FOOD? THERE'S A NEW APPROACH BECKONING.

Food and wine are great dance partners, but this has its limitations, like dancing on stilts. We can see why cocktails don't typically marry with food: alcohol strength, the high cost and labour – but these are all easy to adjust. A cocktail is simply a mixture of liquids, without limitations.

Problems

- Little respect for seasonal and local produce.

- Spirit companies are typically very commercial.

- Adhere too closely to the old formulae, without questioning why.

- Ice machines are used excessively.

- Expensive and don't pair with food.

ZERO WASTE We receive spirits in glass bottles

The cocktail industry has its cultures, styles and expectations. The perception of this industry can limit our vision, so we fail to see the potential. If we shift perspective, we will see that cocktails have a unique potential to match food like no other drink, as they have access to all other liquids, blended into complex layers of bespoke deliciousness.

Cocktails create memorable moments – like a dish, every element can be controlled and personalized, with the added bonus of easing tensions, breaking ice and lubricating conversations.

Solutions

- Seasonal, local perishables.

- Support independent distilleries.

- Embrace alternatives, re-evaluate the formulae and challenge the established set-up.

- Make ice using surplus liquids, or simply chill everything to correct temperatures.

- Lower the ABV (alcohol by volume) to make pairable with food, and bring the cost down accordingly.

that get crushed into glass porcelain.

SEA

INDUSTRIAL FISHING IS RAPIDLY DESTROYING THE OCEANS THROUGH THE EXPLOITATION OF NATURAL RESOURCES.

We are now facing prominent overfishing, ocean pollution and destructive fishing practices, such as trawling – a non-selective practice that destroys marine habitats and creates enormous waste. Meanwhile, the demand for fish is rising dramatically. The natural way is to work with the rhythm of the ocean, taking only what is adequately self-regenerative while ensuring the integrity of the underwater ecosystems. Hook-and-line fishing means there's little or no environmental damage, and no unwanted bycatch. This is also true of some netting and potting (mostly shellfish).

Fish farming has the potential to meet the rising demand. However, like regular farming, this can be done very badly – spreading diseases and sea lice, destroying environments. A fish farm can look to solve one problem only by creating another.

Industrial fishing
- Catches with big nets dredging or trawling
- Catches everything that goes in the net
- Huge fishing tankers
- Fish farming
- Indirect trade

Natural fishing
- Catches with hook and line
- Catches fish that has spawned multiple times
- Small boats (under 10 metres/33 feet in size)
- Careful fishing in harmony with population dynamics
- Direct trade

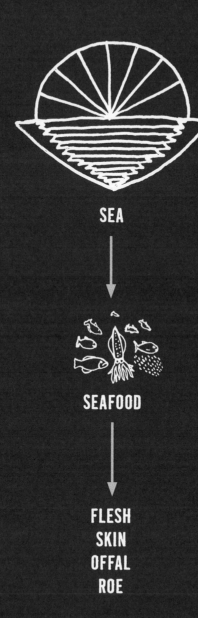

SEA

SEAFOOD

FLESH
SKIN
OFFAL
ROE

SHIP

COFFEE & CHOCOLATE

BEANS
NIBS
CHAFF
BUTTER

SHIP

HOW DO WE RETHINK THE BULK TRANSPORTATION OF EXOTIC INGREDIENTS THAT WE ALL LOVE BUT THAT CAN'T BE GROWN WHERE WE LIVE?

You could go fundamentalist and just do without such exotica, but that is not a solution for everyone. At the moment, such ingredients travel on huge container ships or make faster, costlier (in all senses of the word) journeys by air. Is there another way? A less wasteful way? Well, yes, there is one organization that has stood back and asked: what is there an abundance of? And the answer is that 71% of the planet is covered in seawater. And what is the cheapest, cleanest power source we have? Wind. For centuries, sea freight meant sail power.

Three Dutchmen decided to take a step back to make a leap forward and established Fairtransport, the world's first modern emission-free shipping company. Silo gets coffee via Fairtransport – it still has to be transported from the landing port, but it is a huge saving on energy. It's a fine example of imaginative thinking. The small fleet of traditional sailing ships used by Fairtransport includes the world's only engineless sailing cargo ship. The focus is on transporting special products which are organic or crafted traditionally – such as olive oil, wine and rum. In addition, the fleet is raising awareness of the huge amounts of pollution created by the modern shipping industry and is affecting positive change in the way goods are shipped around the world.

WILD

WILD FOOD IS SYMBOLIC OF THE PALEO/PRIMAL DIET, WHICH IS DEFINED AS PRE-AGRICULTURE. SILO IS PRO-AGRICULTURE, AND THE RATIONALE BEHIND THESE EVOLUTIONARY PRINCIPLES IS VERY PERTINENT.

Diet isn't at the top of our agenda. However, our agenda is to cook food the way that nature intends, and that's the most supreme diet of all. Wild food is the most nutritious of them all.

Our restaurant dwelling is circled with abundant wild plants that nobody else forages. An untapped bounty of produce offering us endless gastronomic opportunities. Wherever you are in the world, even in urban jungles, foraging wild food is available to you, in every season.

Foraging offers far more than culinary wild treats, it's a connection to nature. If foraging was a subject taught at schools, we would have a very different society – I perhaps wouldn't be writing this book if that was a thing. Off-grid food is a niche idea to mainstream society, which is ironic, considering that humans are foragers, as decided by our evolution.

Wild food is the most fundamental food of all. It has a broad range of effects: it can nourish you, it can heal you, it can kill you, it can make you see the world differently.

WILD

WILD PLANTS

ROOTS
BULBS
LEAVES
FLESH
STEM
FLOWERS & SEEDS

FARM

FRUIT & VEGETABLES

SKIN
FLESH
TOPS
STEM
LEAVES & ROOTS

FARM

WHEN WE CHANGE THE WAY WE GROW OUR FOOD, WE CHANGE OUR FOOD, WE CHANGE OUR SOCIETY, WE CHANGE OUR VALUES. SILO MEANS TO SYNTHESIZE OUR OFFERING WITH THE FLOW OF THE FARM.

At the core of natural farming is good soil, considered as a bank account in which the more you invest, the more you have to withdraw. Good soil means good produce. We work with farms where everything grows outside and in season. No pesticides are used, as they deplete the soil. Nor are any artificial fertilizers used – instead, manure is used for mulching after harvesting.

Crop rotation is like an agricultural symphony, one that dictates our menu. Farms are managed as self-sustaining whole organisms; an integrated ecosystem that pays attention to natural rhythms and in which everything supports everything else to create fruitful abundance – nothing gets wasted.

Industrial farming cycle
- Chemical fertilizers and pesticides deplete the soil
- The depleted soil produces devitalized food
- 'Dead' food does not sustain human health
- Resources are wasted on curing/managing self-inflicted disease

This is waste on an industrial scale.

Natural farming cycle
- Naturally fertile soil produces healthy food
- Healthy food produces healthy people
- Resources can be concentrated where needed most
- Resources are not wasted

DAIRY

THE CONCEPT OF EATING THE BREAST MILK OF ANOTHER SPECIES IS QUITE ABSURD, WHEN YOU REALLY THINK ABOUT IT. OVER HALF THE WORLD IS INTOLERANT TO DAIRY, EVEN THOUGH THEY MIGHT NOT KNOW IT.

Dairy is a relatively modern phenomenon in the human diet. With less than a thousand years of consumption under its belt, dairy began in Northern Europe, which, notably, is now the place most adapted to the product. Africa and East Asia have eaten dairy for considerably less time, and, unremarkably, have a greater level of intolerance.

The subject of consuming dairy begs lots of big questions around naturalism, without any clear answer. I don't think any hedonist (in their right mind) would ever say that cheese isn't delicious – it really does make life better. But cheese is made all the more agreeable when used sparingly, and from the life of an animal living on its natural diet in its natural habitat, namely grazing its whole life, not just for a bit.

The crucial point to highlight is that Silo adopts Neolithic pro-agricultural principles. When you consider feeding the human population, foraging is not an option; we need agriculture.

DAIRY

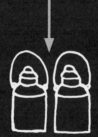

**MILK &
CREAM**

BUTTER
FRESH CHEESE
YOGHURT
SOUR CREAM
WHEY & BUTTERMILK

REWILDING

MEAT

BLOOD
BONES
SKIN
FLESH
OFFAL

REWILDING

PROVIDING AN ALTERNATIVE SOURCE OF MEAT, REWILDING IS A LOW-CARBON, SLOW-FARMING WAY OF RETURNING EXHAUSTED ARABLE LAND TO NATURAL PRODUCTIVITY.

That does not mean leaving the land to run wild, but working with it in a carefully conceived, well-placed, well-managed way. Everyone benefits: the wildlife, the soil, local water supplies and people. Fertilizers and chemicals are banned, and ploughs and intensive sheep grazing are banished. Natural water systems are restored. Slowly, a whole range of different species is introduced, to co-habit the land and create biodiversity.

The consequence is that the land is rich with life, bringing back so many endangered species slowly disappearing, to flourish once again in a safe, sustainable place. Rewilding is about letting go – allowing nature to take control. Standing back, with no expectations, and letting the environment heal. Nature, we are learning, is often far more resilient than we give it credit.

Rewilding is a system symbolic to Silo, a win-win with nature. This is ultimately the most ethical, sustainable, natural origin for meat. This habitat produces a large amount of meat in the name of biodiversity. The meat must die for the greater good of the land.

And that's the rewilding mantra: we must give nature as much, or more, than we take.

THOUGHT PROCESS

CREATIVITY IS A CRUCIAL PART OF ALL DEVELOPMENT AND IDEAS – INESCAPABLE CHALLENGES GRAPPLING THE UNKNOWN.

When you commit to an idea, you will inevitably face countless challenges that can only be overcome with creativity. A new idea can be a gauntlet for self-confidence; self-doubt and irrational behaviour are part of the process. To anticipate and understand the psychology of creative thought is a valuable preparation, which can navigate you through the anxious waters of progress.

The irrational psychology of creative ideas:
1 This idea is amazing.
2 This idea isn't easy.
3 This idea is rubbish.
4 I'm rubbish.
5 Actually, this is quite good.

LOGIC FILTER
The idea can be rationally filtered through a series of logical questions. It's a quick exercise that will help you see more clearly and makes it memorable. For example, making brown cheese from whey: how perishable is brown cheese? What are the *economics* of producing it? Is the process *efficient*? Is this product *pertinent* to me or my business? Is it *desirable*? Logical planning is crucial for Zero Waste. The foresight reveals what needs to happen: to execute efficiently with minimal waste of time, money, energy and materials.

The rational development of logical ideas:
1 A new idea is…?
2 What we know for a fact about this idea.
3 Forget everything that is not a fact.
4 Develop value based on the facts.
5 Execute valuable idea.

INFORMATION

THE CREATIVE FILTER

IDEAS

PERISHABILITY   YIELD   ECONOMICS   THE LOGIC FILTER   EFFICIENCY   PERTINENCE   DESIRABILITY

PRODUCT

THE SILO FOOD SYSTEM

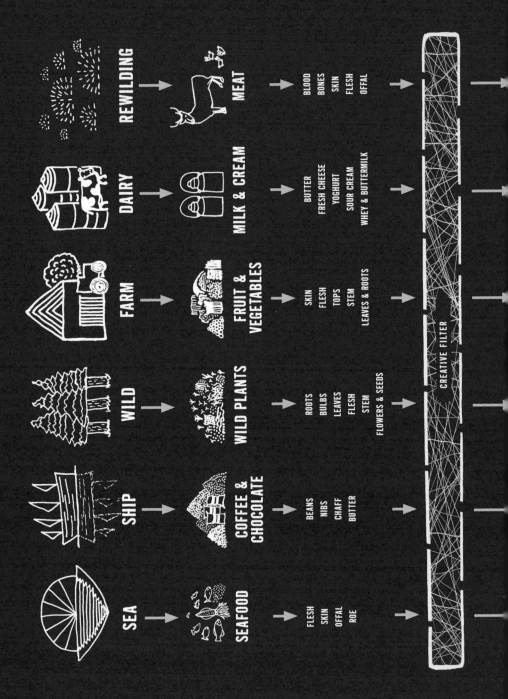

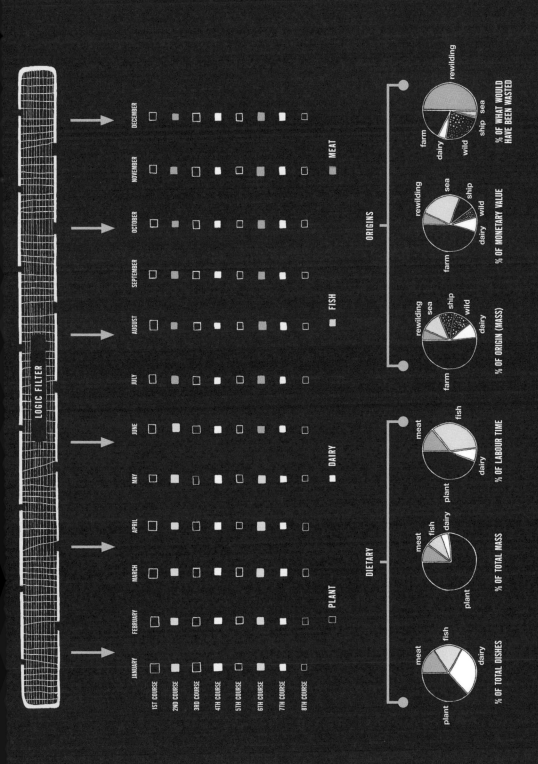

3

FORMULA

THE SILO FORMULA

OUR FOOD FORMULA IS THE SILO HYPOTHESIS IN THE FLESH. IT'S GREAT TO INTELLECTUALIZE POSITIVE IDEAS, BUT MAKING THEM WORK IN REALITY IS HOW WE CAN CHANGE THE WORLD.

Recipes are wonderful things, a guide in the name of consistency. Alas, they are made possible by the very force this book means to counter: industrialism. A recipe works when its variables match those of its initial conception. Industrialism gives us two products that are the same; nature does not.

With this in mind, we offer an alternative: a guide that accommodates the organic curves of real food. We try to do this in a manner considered 'beautiful', because when doing the right thing becomes sexy, the game changes. This is more obviously expressed through the arts of Silo: the language can easily be poetic and the aesthetics can be vistas.

Less obvious is the internal beauty of the system. The efficiency of Silo is a unique quality that commonly gets demoted in the attention of others. As the introduction to this book foretold, Zero Waste is a web of nature, everything is connected. Nature is an irregular force that puts pressure on the system. To ensure the web does not break, there are adaptable formulas we have created, tested and evolved.

Every element of the final dish is weighed out. By having this exact formula we can work backwards, scaling up our production depending on the quantity of the specific ingredients. This foresight means we know where we are going – we can avoid creating waste and avoid wasting time. Most importantly, we do this so we can consistently execute the dish to the highest standard, knowing exactly how we want it to be.

ZERO WASTE

BASIC INGREDIENTS

The Zero Waste solution to basic ingredients is simple:

- **Non-perishables** (dry goods) Buy whole ingredients in bulk, as the packaging is mostly thick paper bags, which are composted.
- **Perishable ingredients** Buy whole ingredients directly from their origin. When milk and cream come directly from the dairy, there is an opportunity to specify the vessel which they occupy. Alternatively, choose items without packaging. If you don't want to make your own butter, find someone who does, with reusable vessel specifications (likewise with yoghurt, cheese and so on).

In an alternative Zero Waste reality, we would have bulk food markets with dispensers to fill reusable vessels. When opening a Zero Waste business take heed: the initial financial outlay can be massive! Vessels, storage space and equipment can cripple your budget. If you're hardcore and want no plastic then it goes to the next level. Consider the cost of reusable plastic vs reusable stainless steel x 1,000; your eyes will water.

Production equipment needs to be factored in, too. Zero Waste dairy and meat are especially sensitive to this consideration. Take butter, for an example: to efficiently and economically sustain production, it must be done in bulk. You then require a big (expensive) mixer. Furthermore, you must consider the space this needs, plus the bulk products being stored effectively in expensive refrigeration.

Thankfully, there are HUGE positives to buying in bulk:

- **It's economically superior** A flour mill will pay for itself, the cost of wholewheat is a fraction of flour and takes a very minor amount of labour to produce. Tip it in the silo, twist the nob and press the button.

- **It's carbon friendly** Consider the journey made just twice a year vs every few weeks. Then multiply this by all the bakers/restaurants in the world.
- **It boosts efficiency in the kitchen** Ordering in bulk means you will always have the product when you need it, rather than relying on ordering daily top-ups.

Salt One of the exceptions to the bulk-buying rule. Its bulk form usually means a big tough plastic bag (single use). There are a number of salts that can be bought in containers that we really need for kitchen storage. You can also buy bricks of salt.

Sugar Can easily be bought in 10–20-kilo (22–44-lb) paper sacks. We went through a sugar-free phase, which made it even easier. I digress. It's nice to use alternative sugars – dark brown sugar is such an underrated flavour. You can also buy malt barley in big reusable containers.

Nuts, seeds and spices Super-easy to buy in bulk paper bags; however, the cost of 10–20 kilos (22–44 lb) of nuts is a huge investment.

Flour Mill your own. Life gets so much better after this. Wholewheat in bulk always comes in paper sacks.

Milk and cream Cow juice comes in a stainless steel pale. You can also use food-grade jerry cans, but they are much harder to clean.

Butter, yoghurt, cultured cream, cheese Make yourself. The bigger the production, the better. If you don't want to make your own; find someone who does, with reusable vessel specifications.

Fish and meat Buy the whole beast; pre-processed animals are wrapped in plastic, but not when they're whole. Be aggressive against polystyrene in particular – there are plenty of returnable containers that will work well for both the fishermen and the chefs. If it's a one-way courier delivery of fish (not ideal), then find the single-use mushroom alternatives to polystyrene. (At the point of writing this, we have not tested them.)

ZERO WASTE

BASIC MATERIALS

The Zero Waste solution to basic materials is simple: buy in bulk, in reusable containers.

I say this is simple, but that's a lie; it's been my ultimate headache. Especially finding a decent oven cleaner. Bulk cleaning products can be found easily from package-free stores, but, unfortunately, behind the scenes, the containers giving you refills are themselves single use. After a never-ending search I found a company that made little cornstarch pouches of cleaning product delivered in big reusable containers. This meant we had a nice collection of big durable containers that cost nothing.

Cleaning implements such as cloths, sponges and cleaning paper are relatively straightforward. Choose biodegradable and find a good brand that doesn't dissolve as you're using it. Buy in bulk, use wisely, maintain quality by soaking regularly in vinegar water, use rigorously until totally exhausted. Only use single-use kitchen cloth for oil spills – this is compostable, but be sensitive to the fate of that compost.

Chefs are terribly wasteful when cleaning kitchens, flooding the kitchen with buckets of hot soapy water, then using vast swathes of kitchen roll that pervade the bin space. The first thing I teach my new staff/stagiaires is how to clean a bench. Use hot soapy water, clean the bench as normal, then use the cloth/sponge to soak up all the moisture, squeezing back into the bucket from which it came, until all the moisture has gone. Finish by sanitizing with vinegar water, using the same 'sponging' method. This means you use no single-use kitchen roll and fill no bin space.

There are other alternative ways of cleaning with Zero Waste:

- **Make your own products** Soap is easy-ish, we did this until we realized it was financially unsustainable on our small scale. That's not to say it won't work for you. Another easier product is sanitizer spray – take a large amount of distilled vinegar and leave lemons in there for a few months to infuse. Then dilute the liquid one part vinegar to five parts water. It will work great and smell incredible.
- **Jesus water** Also know as E-water. It's a process of tap water going through reverse osmosis, then getting electrolyzed to split the pH into extreme states of acid and alkali, killing 99.99999% of bacteria. This Jesus water can be used for all cleaning tasks, including degreasing. We had this set up in the first few years, but unfortunately the machine broke before it made financial sense. It was a crying shame, as this was one of the most remarkable Zero Waste systems imaginable.

SINGLE USE/DISPOSABLES

Cling film Don't use it. Invest in containers with decent lids and buy lots, so you never run out. There is a really good beeswax clingfilm that's endlessly reusable but it's not airtight. There's also a biodegradable clingfilm that doesn't biodegrade – it's best to avoid this until a significant evolution in bioplastics occurs. In those instances when you need to wrap a particular item, use heavy-duty, reusable, zip-seal bags.

Foil Don't use it. Instead, invest in suitable metal lids for the trays you need to cover.

Baking parchment Invest in lots of reusable rubber mats. Treat them with love so they last forever.

Kitchen roll Buy in bulk, find where they're packaged and beg the team to put them loose in the box for you; it won't be above board but do it anyway. Only use for oil spills/grease, very sparingly, and then compost.

Sous vide Don't use it. Replace sous-vide cooking with low-temperature poaching, 'a bath within a bath'. A heavy-duty zip-seal is the last resort.

THE MENUS

WITH OUR DIRECT, WHOLE FOOD SUPPLY CHAIN WE HAVE EVOLVED A UNIQUE APPROACH TO COOKING. ZERO WASTE IS NOT ONLY THE RIGHT THING TO DO, IT'S THE MOST DELICIOUS – WITH NO COMPROMISE.

These pages explain certain pivotal measures we rely on for consistency, adaptability and excellence.

Salt The general seasoning for most raw ingredients is usually around the 1% mark. It's a detail that isn't given enough attention in kitchens, with chefs inconsistently dusting food with a scattering of salt. The method we use for seasoning ingredients (that we are going to cook) is: add 0.5% salt to the raw ingredient, cook, taste, then finish with coarse salt up to an additional 0.5%. Note that all plants, meats, dairy and liquids vary, and the above is just a guide. Of course, any plants from the sea are already salty.

Acidity Throughout the cooking methods, we specify to 'acidify' after cooking an ingredient. Salt is relatively universal; acidity is more subjective. It may be personal as to how you want the dish to taste. The choice of acidity may vary depending on your place in the world. Another crucial consideration is the pH: apple cider vinegar, for example, has a pH of 2.4–3.0, whereas a lemon is more acidic at 2.0. We recommend close attention to acidity: weigh the raw ingredient, weigh the vinegar, work out a percentage and apply when the ingredient is cooked.

A REFERENCING KEY
The specific recipes of the dishes are highlighted in bold on the monthly menu pages and bunched together into categories in the following sections after the menu pages: **Plant Preparations • Ferments, Pickles & Preserves • Stocks, Sauces & Oils • Meat, Fish & Dairy • Nuts, Grains, Seeds & Sweet Things • Ice Creams & Sorbets**

These recipes are explained in parts and percentages (see below), rather than as a finite recipe. Again, this is for efficiency – nature is always giving you different quantities of different shapes with different behaviours. Working out how to cook something should be relative to the produce, not a preordained recipe.

This book is a dedicated overview of our food system, it is not a cookbook – we don't want to prescribe how to put ingredients on plate. There is a great level of detail not documented in our formula; this begs for intuition and a personal touch – crucial for Jedi cooking.

Parts and percentages

We calculate our food quite differently from traditional recipes, so it's not immediately obvious how our method works. However, when you get used to it, it's far more intuitive, versatile and scalable. Furthermore, it can be tailored to a particular ingredient that needs to be used.

Take this scenario: A farmer gives us 4kg (8lb 13oz) of raspberries as a gift. They are starting to go soft, they won't last another day. So, to prevent wasting the raspberries, you choose to make a sorbet. A traditional recipe may ask for 3.2kg (7lb), which means you spend ages altering the recipe or you waste 800g (1lb ¾oz) of raspberries. Our sorbet recipe easily adapts to any quantity as it's all in parts and percentages.

Example:
4 parts fruit (raspberries)
1 part water
1 part light brown sugar

5% glucose
2% dextrose
1% glycerine
0.3% salt

Note: The percentages are worked out based on the total mass of all parts of the base recipe. For example, if you have 4kg (8lb 13oz) raspberries, 1 litre/kg/2lb 3¼oz water, 1kg (2lb 3¼oz) sugar then you are working to the percentages of a 6kg (13¼lb) total mass.

JANUARY
FEBRUARY
MARCH
APRIL
MAY
JUNE
COURSE 1
COURSE 2
COURSE 3
COURSE 4
COURSE 5
COURSE 6
COURSE 7
COURSE 8

JULY AUGUST SEPTEMBER OCTOBER NOVEMBER DECEMBER

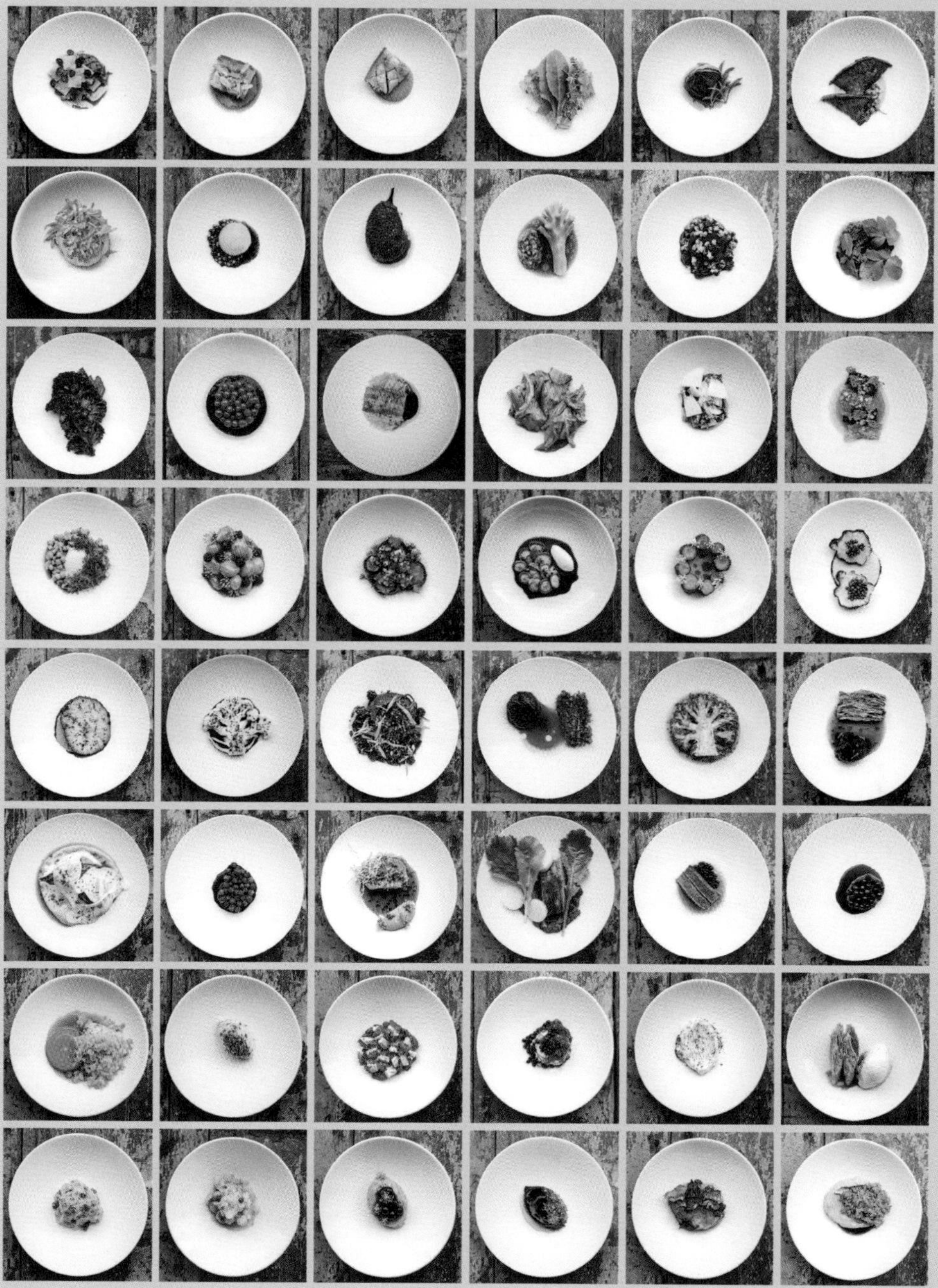

JANUARY

Total menu weight: 732.5g (1lb 9¾oz) **Plant:** 627.5g (1lb 6¼oz) / 85%
Dairy: 35g (1¼oz) / 5% **Fish:** 70g (2½oz) / 10%

JANUARY IS A GREAT MONTH IN ENGLAND. WE HAVE ALL THE APPLES, SEXY CABBAGES, THE BEST RHUBARB IN THE WORLD AND THE ALMIGHTY ALEXANDER PLANT.

1 | Red flesh apples, sourdough miso & sea beet

- Peel, core and steam the apples until tender, not soft.
- Juice the sea beet, acidify and split with soft herb oil.

40g (1⅜oz) peeled, cored apples / 1g (0.035oz) sea beet / 12g (⅜oz) dressing / 3g (0.1oz) **sourdough miso**

2 | Hokkaido pumpkin, forced rhubarb & British sumac

- Steam slices of pumpkin until tender, dress in smoked oil and 0.5–1% salt.
- Dice the rhubarb into 1mm (1/32in) cubes.

55g (2oz) pumpkin / 15g (½oz) diced rhubarb / 15g (½oz) **pumpkin seed butter** / 6g (⅕oz) beach herbs / 0.5g (0.02oz) sumac

3 | Pointy cabbage, onion juice & plaice caviar

- Steam the pointy cabbage heart until tender, season with 0.5–1% salt.
- Whisk caviar through fermented onion juice.

80g (2⅞oz) pointy cabbage / 20g (¾oz) **fermented onion juice** / 10g (⅓oz) caviar / 4g (⅛oz) **tarragon oil**

4 | Chervil root, apple, whey & miso

- Steam the chervil roots whole in their skin until tender, peel by hand and season with 0.5–1% salt.
- Heat up an appropriate amount of reduced whey (see page 135), add a third its weight in butter. In a separate pan, on a high heat, caramelize in small batches until the sauce is silky with a butterscotch colour.
- Core and slice the apple 2mm (1/16in) thick.

40g (1⅜oz) chervil root / 10g (⅓oz) apple / 15g (½oz) caramelized whey sauce / 4g (⅛oz) **sourdough miso**

5 | Shiitake mushrooms, dumplings & mustard

- Fry the dumplings at 180°C (350°F) until they are a light golden colour.
- Roast the mushrooms at 200°C (400°F) for 3 minutes (depending on size).
- Dress with smoked oil, vinegar and 0.5–1% salt.

60g (2⅛oz) raw mushrooms / 60g (2⅛oz) **potato dumplings** / 20g (¾oz) **blue cheese sauce** (vegetarian) or **mustard** sauce (vegan)

6 | Dab, alexander buds & seaweed

- Portion the cured dab.
- Poach the fish in neutral oil at 50°C (120°F), until the internal temperature reaches 46°C (115°F).
- Steam the alexander buds until tender, acidify with bright vinegar and 0.5–1% salt.

60g (2⅛oz) **cured fish** / 30g (1oz) alexander buds / 2g (0.07oz) dried sea lettuce flakes / 2g (0.07oz) **alexander oil**

7 | Rhubarb, alexander flower & sour cream

- Make a stock syrup by whisking 4 parts sugar: 6 parts water to dissolve the sugar.
- Cut the rhubarb, poach in the stock syrup at 65°C (149°F) until tender but still firm, then take off the heat and leave to cool.
- Break up the frozen sour cream into bitesize pieces.

40g (1⅜oz) poached rhubarb / 20g (¾oz) **frozen sour cream** / 10g (⅓oz) rhubarb poaching liquor / 2g (0.07oz) **alexander oil** / 1g (0.035oz) alexander flowers

8 | Alexander & cacao butter ice cream, oil & fresh shoots

80g (2⅞oz) **alexander & cacao butter ice cream** / 8g (¼oz) **caramelized oats** / 4g (⅛oz) **alexander oil** / 2–3 fresh alexander shoots

FEBRUARY

Total menu weight: 747g (1lb 10½oz) **Plant:** 567g (1¼lb) / 76%
Dairy: 60g (2⅛oz) / 8% **Fish:** 120g (4¼oz) / 16%

THIS MENU IS ALL ABOUT THE PEASANT FOOD: BEETROOT, POTATO AND SEAWEED, TOPPED OFF BY BRITAIN'S MOST EVIL INVADER – THE AMERICAN SIGNAL CRAYFISH.

1 | Beetroot, apple & elderberry capers

- Select a large beetroot prune hydrated in sour apple juice, slice one large 40g (1⅜oz) piece and lightly rub in beetroot molasses and 0.5–1% salt.
- Peel, core and steam the cooking apples until cooked and soft. Squeeze the excess juice through a muslin cloth, chop the apple compote until it is a fine pulp.

40g (1⅜oz) **beetroot prune** / 1g (0.035oz) **beetroot molasses** /10g (⅓oz) apple pulp / 10g (⅓oz) **elderberry capers** / 6g (⅕oz) sour apple juice / 5g (⅕oz) olive oil

2 | Potato, kelp & alexander flowers

- Boil waxy potatoes and season with 0.5–1% salt.
- Braise kelp, then slice.

60g (2⅛oz) potatoes / 20g (¾oz) **fermented potato sauce** / 8g (¼oz) **braised kelp** / 1g (0.035oz) alexander flowers

3 | Crayfish & stonecrop

- Put live crayfish on ice for 15 minutes, then boil in 4% brine for about 2 minutes (depending on size). Plunge into ice water.
- Peel the tails, keeping the biggest attached to the body.

40g (1⅜oz) crayfish flesh / 8g (¼oz) **crayfish sauce** / 3g (0.1oz) stonecrop / 3g (0.1oz) **crayfish oil**

4 | Shiitake mushrooms, brown butter & three-cornered garlic

- Roast the mushrooms at 200°C (400°F) for 3 minutes (depending on size).
- Dress with smoked oil, vinegar and 0.5–1% salt.

80g (2⅞oz) raw mushrooms / 10g (⅞oz) **brown butter solids** / 1g (0.035oz) three-cornered garlic flowers / 2g (0.07oz) **three-cornered garlic oil**

5 | Golden beetroot, potato dumplings & lemon thyme

- Steam the beetroots, peel, then roast slowly at 160°C (320°F), add 0.5–1% salt.
- Fry the dumplings at 180°C (350°F) until they are a light golden colour, add 0.5–1% salt.
- Create ribbons of beetroot with a Japanese slicer to 1-mm (1/32-in) thickness, acidify with sweet vinegar and 0.5–1% salt.

40g (1⅜oz) roasted golden beetroot / 10g (⅓oz) beetroot ribbons / 60g (2⅛oz) **potato dumplings** / 25g (⅞oz) **blue cheese sauce** or 20g (¾oz) **mustard dressing** / 1g (0.035oz) lemon thyme / 3g (0.1oz) **lemon thyme oil**

6 | Brill, onion & gooseberry

- Portion the cured brill, keeping it on the bone.
- Grill the fish on both sides to gain a crispy skin, then gently cook until the internal temperature reaches 48°C (118°F).

80g (2⅞oz) **cured fish** / 30g (1oz) **fermented onion & juice** / 10g (⅓oz) **preserved gooseberries**

7 | Rhubarb, cacao toffee, 70% fat cream & Douglas fir

- Ball the toffee into pea-sized shapes, fold through the cream to 1:10 ratio.
- Slice the rhubarb into 1mm (1/32 in)-thick, 25mm (1in)-long slices.

50g (1¾oz) toffee cream / 30g (1oz) rhubarb / 5g (⅕oz) **cacao toffee** /10g (⅓oz) **Douglas fir oil**

8 | Pumpkin seed ice cream, fig leaf & oats

80g (2⅞oz) **pumpkin seed ice cream** / 12g (⅜oz) **caramelized oats** / 4g (⅛oz) **fig leaf oil**

MARCH

Total menu weight: 743g (1lb 10¼oz) **Plant:** 533g (1lb 2¾oz) / 72%
Dairy: 90g (⅜oz) / 12% **Fish:** 120g (4¼oz) / 16%

HERE WE PROUDLY DOUBLE UP ON FISH AND FUNGUS. WHEN YOUR SUPPLY CHAIN IS LIMITED, YOU MUST DO MORE WITH LESS.

1 | Horse mushroom & mushroom 'papaya' miso

- Roast the mushrooms, acidify with bright vinegar and 0.5–1% salt.
- Glaze and finish with bitter flowers.

50g (1¾oz) raw mushroom / 4g (⅛oz) **mushroom 'papaya' miso** / 1g (0.035oz) bitter flowers

2 | Celeriac & dulse

- Steam the celeriac whole, then peel and tear into rock-shaped portions and season with 0.5–1% salt.
- Pickle the dulse for 4 hours in a 2:1:1 pickle (see page 132). If the dulse is packed in salt, rinse it first until the seasoning is neutral.

60g (2⅛oz) cooked celeriac / 20g (¾oz) **dulse sauce** / 10g (⅓oz) pickled dulse

3 | Plaice, broccoli & oyster

- Dice the cured plaice, dress in oyster emulsion.
- Trim the very tips of the broccoli, dress with bright vinegar and smoked oil.

40g (1⅜oz) plaice / 6g (⅕oz) **oyster emulsion** / 20g (¾oz) broccoli tips

4 | Red cabbage, yoghurt, its whey & three-cornered garlic

- Cut the cabbage through its core into 4 pieces, steam until tender, chill, then blacken the edges on a grill.
- Carefully portion, skewering with pins if necessary.
- Heat up an appropriate amount of reduced yoghurt whey (see page 135), add a third its weight in butter. In a separate pan, on a high heat, caramelize in small batches until the sauce is silky with a dark butterscotch colour.
- Finely slice the green garlic leaves.

60g (2⅛oz) cabbage / 5g (⅕oz) **dehydrated yoghurt** / 10g (⅓oz) caramelized yoghurt whey sauce / 3g (0.1oz) three-cornered garlic flowers and leaves

5 | King oyster mushrooms, celeriac & rosemary

- Create ribbons of celeriac with a Japanese slicer to 1mm (1⁄32in) thickness, acidify with bright vinegar.
- Make celeriac stock with some roasted celeriac trimmings, reduce until it has strong flavour.
- Roast the mushrooms at 200°C (400°F) for 3 minutes (depending on size), then dress with smoked oil, vinegar and 0.5–1% salt.

80g (2⅞oz) raw mushrooms / 15g (½oz) celeriac ribbons / 15g (½oz) **celeriac purée** / 15g (½oz) reduced stock / 5g (⅕oz) **rosemary oil**

6 | Flounder, cabbage & Douglas fir

- Portion the cured flounder, keeping it on the bone.
- Grill the fish on both sides to gain a crispy skin, then gently cook until the internal temperature reaches 48°C (118°F).
- Portion the cabbage, steam until tender and add 0.5–1% salt.

80g (2⅞oz) **cured fish** / 70g (2½oz) cabbage / 5g (⅕oz) **fermented onion juice** / 4g (⅛oz) **Douglas fir oil** /1g (0.035oz) dehydrated pine powder and sesame seeds

7 | Sourdough ice cream & brown butter

80g (2⅞oz) **sourdough ice cream** / 10g (⅓oz) **brown butter solids** / 2g (0.07oz) olive oil

8 | Rhubarb, cacao & lemon thyme

- Make a stock syrup by whisking 4 parts sugar: 6 parts water to dissolve the sugar.
- Cut the rhubarb, poach in stock syrup until tender but still firm, then take off the heat and leave to cool.

50g (1¾oz) **rhubarb sorbet** / 40g (1⅜oz) poached rhubarb / 12g (⅜oz) **caramelized cacao shells** / pinch of lemon thyme

APRIL

Total menu weight: 747g (1lb 10½oz) **Plant:** 582g (1lb 4½oz) / 79%
Dairy: 50g (1¾oz) / 6% **Fish:** 115g (4oz) / 15%

GLOBAL WARMING IS GOING TO CHANGE THINGS – THE WINTER SEASON MAY START STRADDLING THE SPRING.

1 | Hokkaido pumpkin & nasturtium
- Steam slices of pumpkin until tender.
- Dress in olive oil and 0.5–1% salt.

55g (2oz) pumpkin / 15g (½oz) **pumpkin seed praline** / 5g (⅕oz) sour apple juice / 2g (0.07oz) nasturtium / 2g (0.07oz) **nasturtium oil**

2 | Celeriac & kelp
- Steam the celeriac whole, then peel and tear into rock-shaped portions and season with 0.5–1% salt.

60g (2⅛oz) cooked celeriac / 20g (¾oz) **kelp stock** / 10g (⅓oz) **braised kelp** / 1g (0.035oz) three-cornered garlic flowers

3 | Whelks, pointed cabbage & Douglas fir
- Braise the whelks in 2% brine until tender, chill.
- Slice the cooked whelks.
- Portion the cabbage, steam until tender and season with 0.5–1% salt.

35g (1¼oz) whelks / 45g (1½oz) cabbage / 5g (⅕oz) **fermented onion juice** / 3g (0.1oz) **Douglas fir oil** / 1g (0.035oz) dehydrated pine powder and sesame seeds

4 | Potato, sea kale & buttermilk
- Boil waxy potatoes and season with 0.5–1% salt.
- Heat up an appropriate amount of reduced cultured buttermilk (see page 140), add a third of its weight in butter, then caramelize in small batches until lightly golden.
- Chargrill the sea kale and dress lightly with vegetable treacle.

60g (2⅛oz) potatoes / 15g (½oz) caramelized buttermilk sauce / 30g (1oz) sea kale / 1g (0.035oz) bitter flowers / 1g (0.035oz) **vegetable treacle**

5 | Cauliflower, red onion & mustard
- Dice the red onion, then slowly cook in a pan until it breaks down and becomes sweet. Acidify with bright vinegar and 0.5–1% salt.
- Peel the broccoli stem, slice thinly into circles against the grain, blanch until tender.
- Cut the cauliflower through its root, keeping it together in a clean portion. Fry until golden at 180°C (350°F), season with 0.5–1% salt.

70g (2½oz) cauliflower slice / 20g (¾oz) cooked red onion / 15g (½oz) **mustard dressing** / 15g (½oz) sliced broccoli stem / 2g (0.07oz) **marjoram oil** / 1g (0.035oz) marjoram

6 | Plaice, its roe & sea beet
- Portion the cured plaice.
- Poach the fish in neutral oil at 50°C (120°F), until internal temperature reaches 46°C (115°F).

80g (2⅞oz) **cured fish** / 10g (⅓oz) sea beet / dried roe, liberally grated / 4g (⅛oz) **fermented onion juice**

7 | Wholewheat puff pastry, rose & sour cream
- Boil dark brown sugar with water 1:1 ratio, chill to room temperature.

30g (1oz) **wholewheat puff pastry** / 20g (¾oz) **sour cream** / 8g (¼oz) **pickled rose petals** / 5g (⅕oz) rose petal pickling liquor / 5g (⅕oz) dark sugar syrup

8 | Pine & algae ice cream, Douglas fir oil & oats
80g (2⅞oz) **pine & algae ice cream** / 12g (⅜oz) **caramelized oats** / 4g (⅛oz) **Douglas fir oil**

MAY

Total menu weight: 678g (1½lb) Plant: 553g (1lb 3½oz) / 82%
Dairy: 30g (1oz) / 4% Fish: 95g (3⅜oz) / 14%

AS SPRING STARTS KICKING OFF WE WELCOME BRITAIN'S MOST INVASIVE PLANT SPECIES – JAPANESE KNOTWEED.

1 | Purple daikon, walnut & nasturtium
- Slice purple daikon to 4mm (⅛in) slices, weigh and season with 0.5–1% salt.
- Pickle daikon for 1 hour in a 3:2:1 pickle (see page 132).

45g (1½oz) daikon / 15g (½oz) **walnut praline** / 5g (⅕oz) sour apple juice / 2g (0.07oz) nasturtium / 2g (0.07oz) **nasturtium oil**

2 | Tiger green tomatoes, monk's beard & oyster
- Dry the tomato from the brine.
- Pick, blanch and refresh the monk's beard.

50g (1¾oz) **brined tomato** / 10g (⅓oz) **oyster emulsion** / 15g (½oz) monk's beard

3 | Mackerel, dulse & Japanese knotweed
- Slice cured mackerel into 1cm (⅜in)-thick slices.
- Pickle the dulse for 8 hours in a 3:2:1 pickle (see page 132).

45g (1½oz) **cured fish** / 6g (⅕oz) dulse / 4g (⅛oz) **pickled Japanese knotweed** / 4g (⅛oz) dulse pickling liquid

4 | Peas, curds & whey
- Pod the peas, then steam for 1 minute.
- Steam the mange tout for 2 minutes.
- Tumble both together and acidify with bright vinegar, 0.5–1% salt and freshly ground pepper.

50g (1¾oz) peas and mange tout / 10g (⅓oz) whey / 10g (⅓oz) **fresh curd** / 4g (⅛oz) **mint oil** / 4–6 pea flowers

5 | Hen of the woods & Jerusalem artichoke
- Confit the artichokes until tender, chill. Blacken on the grill, chill. Chop into a paste, acidify and dress in smoked oil and 0.5–1% salt.
- Reduce the mushroom stock until thick and intense.

- Roast the mushrooms at 200°C (400°F) for 3 minutes (depending on size) then dress with garlic oil, vinegar and 0.5–1% salt.

80g (2⅞oz) raw mushrooms / 25g (⅞oz) artichoke paste / 8g (¼oz) reduced **mushroom stock** / 3g (0.1oz) **garlic oil**

6 | Wrasse, cauliflower & rock samphire
- Portion the cured wrasse.
- Shave the cauliflower into 2mm (1/16in)-thick slices.
- Boil the black quinoa for 8 minutes, drain, season with 0.5–1% salt and fennel oil.
- Poach the fish in neutral oil at 50°C (120°F) until the internal temperature reaches 46°C (115°F).
- Dress the cauliflower and quinoa in bright vinegar, fennel oil and 0.5–1% salt.
- Steam samphire for 1 minute.

60g (2⅛oz) **cured fish** / 20g (¾oz) cauliflower / 10g (⅓oz) black quinoa / 10g (⅓oz) **cauliflower purée** / 10g (⅓oz) samphire / 3g (0.1oz) fennel oil

7 | Rhubarb, sour cream & elderflower
- Make a stock syrup by whisking 4 parts sugar: 6 parts water to dissolve the sugar.
- Cut the rhubarb, poach in stock syrup until tender but still firm, take off the heat and leave to cool.
- Break up the frozen sour cream into bitesize pieces.

40g (1⅜oz) poached rhubarb / 20g (¾oz) **frozen sour cream** / 10g (⅓oz) rhubarb poaching liquor / 3g (0.1oz) **elderflower oil** / 1g (0.035oz) fresh elderflower

8 | Fig leaf & cacao butter ice cream, fig oil & crystallized leaves
- Steam young fig leaves for 20 seconds, chill, dip in stock syrup at a 1:1 ratio, dry in an 80°C (176°F) oven until crisp.

70g (2½oz) **fig leaf & cacao butter ice cream** / 15g (½oz) crystallized fig leaves / 6g (⅕oz) **fig leaf oil**

JUNE

Total menu weight: 751.5g (1lb 10½oz) **Plant:** 551.5g (1lb 3⅜oz) / 74%
Dairy: 85g (3oz) / 11% **Fish:** 115g (4oz) / 15%

JUNE IS A GOOD MONTH FOR MINIMALISM – SINGLE INGREDIENTS TICKLED IN THE RIGHT WAY – AND OUR BELOVED OYSTERS, SERVED IN A VEGAN COURSE.

1 | Cucumber, oyster & stonecrop

- Defrost and dry the cucumber.

50g (1¾oz) **defrosted salted cucumber** / 10g (⅓oz) **oyster sauce** / 5g (⅕oz) stonecrop / 0.5g (0.02oz) **alexander pollen**

2 | Tomatoes, walnut & rose

- Dry the tomato from the brine.
- Toast the walnuts lightly at 160ºC (320°F).

50g (1¾oz) **brined tomato** / 10g (⅓oz) **walnut butter** / 3g (0.1oz) **rose oil** / 10g (⅓oz) walnuts / fresh rose petals

3 | Crayfish

- Put live crayfish on ice for 15 minutes, then boil in 4% brine for about 2 minutes (depending on size), then plunge into ice water.
- Peel the tails and claws.

45g (1½oz) crayfish / 8g (¼oz) **crayfish sauce** / 4g (⅛oz) **crayfish oil** / 2g (0.07oz) stonecrop

4 | Shallots, brown butter solids & mint

- Roast banana shallots until tender, select the correct-sized onion shells to the appropriate weight, peel the membranes from the onion.
- Fill the shallots with fresh cheese mixed with finely chopped fresh mint, 0.5–1% salt and mint sauce.
- Dress outer surface of shallots with smoked oil and 0.5–1% salt.

55g (2oz) roasted shallots / 15g (½oz) **fresh curd** / 10g (⅓oz) **brown butter solids** / 5g (⅕oz) **mint sauce** / 1g (0.035oz) fresh mint

5 | King oyster mushroom

- Reduce mushroom stock until thick and intense.
- Slice 2mm (1⁄16in)-thick slices of mushroom from the centre.
- Roast the king oyster mushrooms at 200°C (400°F) for 3 minutes (depending on size).
- Dress with smoked oil, vinegar and 0.5–1% salt.

70g (2½oz) king oyster mushrooms / 25g (⅞oz) **duxelles** / 10g (⅓oz) raw mushrooms / 8g (¼oz) reduced **mushroom stock**

6 | Trout, peas & fennel

- Portion the cured trout.
- Poach the fish in neutral oil at 50°C (120°F) until internal temperature reaches 44°C (111°F).
- Steam the peas very briefly and acidify with bright vinegar and 0.5–1% salt.

70g (2½oz) **cured fish** / 50g (1¾oz) peas / 12g (⅜oz) **pea purée** / 3g (0.1oz) **fennel oil** / fennel fronds

7 | Goat's cheese, lavender & oats

60g (2⅛oz) **goat's cheese ice cream** / 50g (1¾oz) **oat paste** / 8 small buds fresh lavender

8 | Elderflower & cacao butter ice cream

80g (2⅞oz) **elderflower & cacao butter ice cream** / 4g (⅛oz) **elderflower oil** / 2g (0.07oz) **preserved elderflower**

JULY

Total menu weight: 680g (1½lb) **Plant:** 510g (1lb 2oz) / 76%
Dairy: 35g (1¼oz) / 5% **Meat:** 135g (4¾oz) / 19%

AS WE SWITCH FROM FISH TO MEAT, WE START BY SERVING THE FRESH CUTS, ALLOWING THE REST OF THE ANIMAL TO AGE FOR THE NEXT MONTH.

1 | Potato, blackcurrant & pineapple weed

- Slice waxy potatoes into 1mm (1/32 in)-thick slices, then boil until just cooked.
- Pat dry, dress with pineapple weed oil and 0.5–1% salt.

35g (1¼oz) boiled potatoes / 15g (½oz) **fermented potato skin** / 2g (0.07oz) pineapple weed / 3g (0.1oz) **pineapple weed oil** / 10g (⅓oz) blackcurrant / 8g (¼oz) blackcurrant juice

2 | Pineapple tomato, hazelnut butter & marigold

- Slice a 1cm (⅜in)-thick wedge through the centre of the tomato, season with 0.5–1% salt.

40g (1⅜oz) pineapple tomatoes / 15g (½oz) **hazelnut butter** / 2g (0.07oz) **marigold oil** / 2g (0.07oz) **tomato brine**

3 | Sheep heart, kale & red grapes

- Grill individual muscles of sheep heart to 54°C (129°F), season with 0.5–1% salt.
- Pour a small amount of sheep stock over the heart in a small bowl to collect the resting juices and make a sauce.
- Once rested, slice the heart into 3mm (3/32 in)-thick slices.
- Grill the red kale quickly over a high heat, then dress with smoked oil and vinegar.

55g (2oz) sheep heart / 35g (1¼oz) kale / 10g (⅓oz) **sliced fermented grapes** / 10g (⅓oz) **resting juice** sauce

4 | Peas, fresh curd & mint

- Pod the peas, steam for 1 minute, acidify with bright vinegar, 0.5–1% salt and freshly ground pepper.
- Finely slice the mint with a sharp knife.

25g (7/8oz) peas / 10g (⅓oz) **fresh curd** / 1g (0.035oz) mint / 3g (0.1oz) **mint oil**

5 | Celeriac glazed in treacle, kelp & elderberry

- Steam whole celeriac to an internal temperature of 80°C (176°F), peel the skin, glaze in vegetable treacle and slowly bake, reapplying treacle to build crust.
- Portion the celeriac and season with 0.5–1% salt.

60g (2⅛oz) celeriac / 20g (¾oz) **kelp sauce** / 10g (⅓oz) **pickled elderberries**

6 | Retired sheep, patty pans & marjoram

- Slice the patty pans on a mandolin to 1mm (1/32 in)-thick neat slices, add 0.5–1% salt.

80g (2⅞oz) **braised sheep** / 15g (½oz) **patty pan purée** / 15g (½oz) patty pan slices / 10g (⅓oz) **braising juices** / 4g (⅛oz) **marjoram oil** / 1g (0.035oz) fresh leaves

7 | Sea buckthorn, brown butter & Douglas fir

35g (1¼oz) **sea buckthorn jelly** / 15g (½oz) 70% cream / 10g (⅓oz) **Douglas fir oil** / 8g (¼oz) **frozen sea buckthorn** / 10g (⅓oz) **brown butter solids**

8 | Green & red gooseberries & elderflower

- Slice ripe gooseberries into 2mm (1/16 in)-thick slices.
- Boil dark brown sugar with water 1:1 ratio, chill to room temperature.

60g (2⅛oz) **red gooseberry sorbet** / 30g (1oz) sliced green gooseberries / 5g (⅕oz) dark sugar syrup / 4g (⅛oz) **elderflower oil** / 2g (0.07oz) **preserved elderflower**

AUGUST

Total menu weight: 561.5g (1lb 3¾oz) **Plant:** 386.5g (13½oz) / 68%
Dairy: 35g (1¼oz) / 6% **Meat:** 140g (5oz) / 24%

THE LATE SUMMER IS AN OVERWHELMING ASSAULT OF BERRIES, SOME FRESH BLOOD AND THE AGED SHEEP.

1 | **Cucumber, oyster & marigold**
- Defrost and dry the cucumber.

50g (1¾oz) **defrosted salted cucumber** / 10g (⅓oz) **oyster emulsion** / 0.5g (0.02oz) marigold petals / 2g (0.07oz) **marigold oil**

2 | **Tiger green tomatoes, ripe & unripe elderberries**
- Brine tomatoes (see page 127), with the addition of 1% dried elderflower.
- Juice ripe elderberries.

50g (1¾oz) **brined tomato** / 15g (½oz) **elderberry capers** / 10g (⅓oz) ripe elderberry juice

3 | **Blood pudding, redcurrants & wine**
- Pan-fry the blood pudding until crispy on both sides.

60g (21/8oz) **blood pudding** / 15g (½oz) redcurrants / 8g (¼oz) **red wine reduction**

4 | **Little Linzer potatoes, whey, blackberries & fennel flower**
- Boil potatoes and season with 0.5–1% salt.
- Heat up an appropriate amount of reduced whey (see page 135), add a third of its weight in butter. In a separate pan, on a high heat, caramelize in small batches until the sauce is silky with a butterscotch colour.

55g (2oz) potato / 15g (½oz) whey sauce / 12g (⅜oz) blackberries / 8–10 fennel flowers

5 | **Cauliflower, white onion & black garlic**
- Dice the white onion, slowly cook in a pan until it breaks down and becomes sweet. Acidify with bright vinegar and 0.5–1% salt.
- Cut the cauliflower through the root, keeping it together in a clean portion. Steam until tender, pat dry and season with 0.5–1% salt.
- Chop the lovage with a sharp knife.

70g (2½oz) cauliflower slice / 20g (¾oz) cooked white onion/ 12g (⅜oz) **black garlic paste** / 2g (0.07oz) **lovage oil** / 1g (0.035oz) lovage

6 | **Retired sheep & pickled unripe blackberries**
80g (2⅞oz) **roasted sheep** / 15g (½oz) **pickled unripe blackberries** / 10g (⅓oz) **resting juices**

7 | **Raw cream ice cream & preserved elderflower**
80g (2⅞oz) **raw cream ice cream** / 4g (⅛oz) **elderflower oil** / 3g (0.1oz) **preserved elderflower**

8 | **Gooseberries, sour cream & pineapple weed**
- Make a stock syrup by whisking 4 parts sugar: 6 parts water to dissolve the sugar.
- Poach slightly underripe gooseberries in stock syrup until tender, take off heat and leave to cool.

40g (1⅜oz) **poached gooseberries** / 20g (¾oz) **sour cream** / 8g (¼oz) **frozen pineapple weed** / 3g (0.1oz) **pineapple weed oil** / 1g (0.035oz) fresh pineapple weed

SEPTEMBER

Total menu weight: 668g (1lb 7⅝oz) **Plant:** 503g (1lb 1⅝oz) / 76%
Dairy: 35g (1¼oz) / 5% **Meat:** 130g (4½oz) / 19%

A MONTH OF MEATY TEXTURES, PRECIOUS PRESERVES, FIERCE FLAVOURS AND FENNEL FLOWERS.

1 | Cucumber, oyster & fennel flower
• Defrost and dry the cucumber.

50g (1¾oz) **defrosted salted cucumber** / 10g (⅓oz) **oyster emulsion** / 3–5 fennel flowers

2 | Young aubergine, walnut & British sumac
• Slice the aubergine lengthways to 70g (2½oz), season with 0.5–1% salt, rub with oil and slowly roast until tender. Glaze lightly in vegetable treacle and sumac.
• Cook finely diced shallots in a heavy-based pot with a lid on, until soft and translucent.

60g (2⅛oz) cooked aubergine / 15g (½oz) **walnut praline** / 15g (½oz) shallots / 8g (¼oz) **pickled alexander stem** / 1g (0.035oz) **vegetable treacle** / 1g (0.035oz) sumac

3 | Pig, swede & wine
• Braise the cured pig until tender, then chill, cut and grill.

60g (2⅛oz) **cured pig** / 15g (½oz) **fermented swede** / 10g (⅓oz) **red wine reduction** / 4g (⅛oz) **marjoram oil**

4 | Carrots, egg yolk & stems
• Steam the carrots whole until the temperature reaches 95°C (203°F) in the centre, so they are spongy but still firm.
• Portion the carrots and season with 0.5–1% salt.
• Blend the egg yolks until they reach 62°C (144°F) in the blender, acidify to taste.

60g (2⅛oz) carrots / 15g (½oz) egg yolk / 8g (¼oz) **pickled alexander stems** / 3g (0.1oz) **tarragon oil** / 1g (0.035oz) scurvy grass

5 | Beetroot, blackberry & tarragon
• Create beetroot noodles on a spiralizer, pickle in 3:2:1 pickle (see page 132) overnight.
• Steam whole beetroot, peel, dress with smoked oil and season with 0.5–1% salt.

70g (2½oz) beetroot / 15g (½oz) pickled beetroot noodles / 20g (¾oz) blackberries / 3g (0.1oz) **tarragon oil** / 1g (0.035oz) tarragon

6 | Old pig & vintage parsnips
• Shred raw parsnips into matchsticks, dehydrate at 60°C (140°F) until dry and crisp.

70g (2½oz) **poached pork** / 15g (½oz) **parsnip purée** / 10g (⅓oz) **parsnip gravy** / 5g (⅛oz) dried parsnip / 3g (0.1oz) **fennel oil** / 8–10 fennel flowers

7 | Rosehips, caramelized honey & sour cream
• Freeze Japanese rosehips, defrost, cut into quarters, deseed.

30g (1oz) defrosted rosehips / 10g (⅓oz) **frozen sour cream** / 10g (⅓oz) **caramelized honey** / pinch of **alexander pollen**

8 | Potato skin ice cream, blackcurrant & fennel flower

60g (2⅛oz) **potato skin ice cream** / 10g (⅓oz) blackcurrants / 3–5 fennel flowers

OCTOBER

Total menu weight: 762g (1lb 10¾oz) **Plant:** 567g (1lb 3⅞oz) / 77%
Dairy: 65g (2¼oz) / 8% **Meat:** 120g (4¼oz) / 15%

ANOTHER STRONG MONTH FOR PEASANT COOKING, AND A TRANSITION FROM PORK TO VENISON USING AGED OLD PIG AND FRESH VENISON LIVER.

1 | Hokkaido pumpkin, sour apple juice & beach herbs

- Steam 4mm (⅛in) slices of pumpkin until tender, dress in smoked oil and 0.5–1% salt.
- Juice apple, including trim, and reduce by half.

55g (2oz) pumpkin / 5g (⅕oz) sour apple juice / 15g (½oz) **pumpkin seed praline** / 8g (¼oz) beach herbs

2 | Broccoli & seaweed

- Make purée with all the trim.
- Confit garlic cloves in a pan of neutral oil, slowly until golden and soft. Purée, then add equal parts to the broccoli purée.

60g (2⅛oz) broccoli stem / 18g (⅔oz) **broccoli purée** / 5g (⅕oz) raw broccoli tips / 20g (¾oz) **kelp & mushroom stock**

3 | Venison liver, chard & treacle

- Trim the liver, carefully removing the outer membrane.
- Poach it in a brine made with venison stock and 0.5–1% salt until the internal temperature reaches 54°C (129°F), chill and portion.
- Pan-roast the liver to gain a caramelized crust.
- Pour a small amount of stock over the liver in a small bowl to collect the resting juices and make a sauce.
- Once rested, slice the liver into 4mm (⅛in)-thick slices.
- Grill the chard, then dress with smoked oil, vegetable treacle and vinegar.

50g (1¾oz) liver / 50g (1¾oz) chard / 10g (⅓oz) **resting juices** / 2g (0.07oz) **vegetable treacle**

4 | Baby shiitake mushrooms, mushroom 'papaya' miso & sour cream

- Roast mushrooms, then dress with smoked oil, vinegar and 0.5–1% salt.

60g (2⅛oz) raw mushrooms / 15g (½oz) **sour cream** / 4g (⅛oz) **mushroom 'papaya' miso** / 1g (0.035oz) marjoram leaves

5 | Beetroot, kale & sourdough miso

- Steam beetroot, peel, then dehydrate at 90°C (194°F) for 10–20 hours until prune-like.
- Hydrate the beetroots in mushroom stock with 2% salt for 6–8 hours.
- Steam the kale leaves very briefly, chill. Spread miso lightly over each leaf.
- Stack the kale leaves into a rectangle 10cm x 25cm (4in x 10in), then create a stack 7cm (3in) deep. Press in the fridge for an hour.
- Slice the terrine into a neat 2cm (¾in)-thick wedge and roast at 180°C (350°F) for 2 minutes.
- Take the beetroot out of the stock, roast at 180°C (350°F) for 3 minutes, glaze with beetroot molasses.

60g (2⅛oz) **beetroot prune** / 40g (1⅜oz) terrine / 15g (½oz) **mushroom stock** / 1g (0.035oz) **garlic oil** / 2g (0.07oz) **beetroot molasses**

6 | Old pig & Tokyo turnips

- Blend the raw turnip tops with a small amount of neutral oil (to lubricate the blending) and 1% raw minced garlic. Season lightly with bright vinegar, mustard and sugar.
- Cut the turnip into even pucks and steam until tender.

70g (2½oz) **poached pork** / 15g (½oz) turnip top paste / 20g (¾oz) turnip / 15g (½oz) **pork sauce** / 5g (⅕oz) fresh turnip tops

7 | Miso ice cream, miso caramel & elderberry

50g (1¾oz) **miso ice cream** / 10g (⅓oz) **miso caramel** / 10g (⅓oz) **pickled elderberry** / 8g (¼oz) **frozen elderberry granita**

8 | Blackcurrant, mushroom & alexander pollen

50g (1¾oz) **blackcurrant sorbet** / 10g (⅓oz) **mushroom oil** / pinch of **alexander pollen**

NOVEMBER

Total menu weight: 693g (1lb 8½oz) **Plant:** 498g (1lb 1⅝oz) / 73%
Dairy: 65g (2¼oz) / 9% **Meat:** 130g (4½oz) / 18%

IT'S THE TIME OF YEAR TO TURN UP THE CREATIVITY. HOW LONG CAN WE KEEP SERVING BERRIES FOR...?

1 | Onions glazed in onions
- Slice the onions in half through the root, slowly roast until tender, then dress in treacle made from wasted onion.
- Pickle samphire for 6 hours in a 3:2:1 pickle (see page 132).

50g (1¾oz) roasted onion / 4g (⅛oz) **onion treacle** / 10g (⅓oz) pickled samphire / 4g (⅛oz) fermented onion juice / 3g (0.1oz) **marjoram oil**

2 | Beetroot, blackberry & basil
- Steam and peel the beetroot, season in 0.5–1% salt.

50g (1¾oz) beetroot / 20g (¾oz) **preserved blackberries** / 1g (0.035oz) basil / 2g (0.07oz) **basil oil**

3 | Venison kidney, Tokyo turnip & turnip tops
- Peel off the kidney's membrane and soak for 24 hours in a 2% brine.
- Cut the kidney in half and remove the inner fatty cartilage.
- Pan-roast the kidney, keeping it pink in the middle.
- Pour a small amount of stock over the kidney in a small bowl, to collect the resting juices.
- Juice the turnip tops, acidify slightly and split with smoked oil.
- Slice the turnip into appropriate 2mm (¹⁄₁₆in)-thick pieces.

40g (1⅜oz) kidney / 30g (1oz) Tokyo turnip slices / 8g (¼oz) Tokyo turnip top dressing / 8g (¼oz) **resting juices** / 2g (0.07oz) bitter flowers / 4g (⅛oz) **mustard**

4 | Carrots, egg yolk & stems
- Steam the carrots whole until the temperature reaches 95°C (203°F) in the centre, so they are spongy but still firm.
- Chill, smoke, then chargrill whole carrots.
- Portion the carrots and season with 0.5–1% salt.
- Blend the egg yolks until they reach 62°C (144°F) in the blender, acidify to taste, bottle.

60g (2⅛oz) carrots / 15g (½oz) egg yolk / 3g (0.1oz) **carrot top & garlic oil** / carrot flowers

5 | Cauliflower, lovage & shallots
- Slice the shallots, slowly cook in a pan until they break down and become sweet, acidify with dark vinegar and 0.5–1% salt.
- Cut the cauliflower through the root, keeping together in a clean portion. Fry until golden and tender, season with 0.5–1% salt.
- Chop the lovage with a sharp knife, disperse through lovage oil.

70g (2½oz) cauliflower slice / 20g (¾oz) cooked shallots / 15g (½oz) sliced stem / 3g (0.1oz) **lovage oil** / 1g (0.035oz) lovage

6 | Venison, pickled elderberries & fat
- Mince and render venison fat

80g (2⅞oz) **aged venison** / 15g (½oz) **pickled elderberry** / 15g (½oz) **fermented onion juices** / 10g (⅓oz) rendered fat

7 | Preserved blackberries, sour cream & alexander pollen
- Defrost blackberries so they are soft but still cold, dress in caramelized honey.

50g (1¾oz) sour cream / 10g (⅓oz) **caramelized honey** / 25g (⅞oz) **preserved blackberry** / pinch of **alexander pollen**

8 | Rosehip & roses
70g (2½oz) **rosehip sorbet** / 5g (⅕oz) **rose oil** / pinch of dried roses

DECEMBER

Total menu weight: 721g (1lb 9⅜oz) **Plant:** 568g (1lb 4¼oz) / 80%
Dairy: 63g (2¼oz) / 8% **Meat:** 90g (3⅛oz) / 12%

WITH LOTS OF PRESERVATION AND MUSCULAR VEGETABLES, THE STAGE IS SET FOR A RARE GUEST APPEARANCE – SAFFRON.

1 | Abalone mushrooms & three-cornered garlic

- Roast mushrooms, acidify and dress in garlic oil and 0.5–1% salt.

60g (2⅛oz) raw mushroom / 5g (⅕oz) **preserved three-cornered garlic capers /** 4g (⅛oz) **fermented onion juice**

2 | Aubergine, sunflower seeds & alexander

- Slice, grill and cold-smoke the aubergine.

60g (2⅛oz) aubergine / 15g (½oz) **sunflower seed praline** / 8g (¼oz) **pickled alexander stems** / alexander leaves

3 | Carrots, sheep fat & hogweed seeds

- Mince and render well-aged sheep fat.
- Cook carrots whole in fat until the temperature reaches 95°C (203°F) in the centre, so that they are spongy but still firm.
- Slice the carrots in half lengthways and add 0.5–1% salt.
- Slice the hogweed seed very finely.
- Juice carrots and mix with an equal quantity of aged rendered fat.

55g (2oz) carrots / 15g (½oz) fat and carrot juice dressing / 10g (⅓oz) **linseed brittle** / 1g (0.035oz) hogweed seed

4 | Jerusalem artichoke, stilton & elderberries

- Thoroughly clean the artichokes.
- Slowly roast the artichokes until really soft, then deep-fry until golden and add 0.5–1% salt.

60g (2⅛oz) artichoke / 18g (⅔oz) **blue cheese sauce** / 8g (¼oz) **fermented elderberries** / 2g (0.07oz) **elderberry reduction**

5 | Beetroot, hispi cabbage & potato skin

- Steam the beetroot, peel, then dehydrate at 90°C (194°F) for 10–20 hours until prune-like.
- Hydrate the beetroot in potato skin stock with 2% salt for 6 hours
- Steam the hispi leaves very briefly, chill. Spread potato skin stock lightly over each leaf.
- Stack the cabbage leaves into a rectangle 10cm x 25cm (4in x 10in), then create a stack 7cm (3in) deep. Press in the fridge for an hour.
- Slice the terrine into a neat 2cm (¾in)-thick wedge and roast at 180°C (350°F) for 2 minutes.
- Take the beetroot out of the stock, roast at 180°C (350°F) for 3 minutes, glaze with beetroot molasses.

60g (2⅛oz) **beetroot prune** / 40g (1⅜oz) terrine / 15g (½oz) **potato skin stock /** 1g (0.035oz) **garlic oil** / 2g (0.07oz) **beetroot molasses**

6 | Venison & fermented aronia berry

80g (2⅞oz) **aged venison** / 20g (¾oz) **braising juices** / 20g (¾oz) **pickled aronia berry** / 5g (⅕oz) **elderberry reduction**

7 | Saffron, ice cream & wholewheat puff pastry

- Boil dark brown sugar with water 1:1 ratio, chill.

35g (1¼oz) **saffron ice cream** / 30g (1oz) **wholewheat puff pastry** / 5g (⅕oz) dark sugar syrup

8 | Greengage & malt

55g (2oz) **malt ice cream** / 15g (½oz) **frozen greengages** / 8g (¼oz) **malt toffee**

PLANT PREPARATIONS

THE PURPOSE OF PREPARING ALL OUR
INGREDIENTS IS TO MAKE THEM TASTE THE
BEST VERSION OF THEMSELVES WITH
MINIMAL INTERVENTION, WHILE ALWAYS
PLAYING TO THEIR STRENGTHS.

Alexanders

We give this plant extra attention due to its abundance and because it is rarely used to its full potential. Alexanders can be picked 12 months of the year – they grow fresh through the winter, when little else does.

The annual guide:

- September to October – Serve young shoots and tender stems raw.
- November to December – Preserve and cook large stems and leaves.
- January to February – Roast, fry and steam buds.
- March to April – Serve flowers raw.
- May to June – Serve fresh pollen. This is the most prized stage of the alexanders' life. The overwhelming abundance of this mighty crop means that you can pick enough for a whole year. Gently use a spray tap to rinse the flower head, removing any insects and taking care not to wash the pollen from the plant. The flower formation is the same as fennel flowers. We serve the pollen fresh for as long as we can, then to preserve it we use scissors, separating the individual flowers to almost the consistency of sand and drying them on trays at room temperature. It takes a long time, but then it's a very precious product.
- July to August – Alexanders hibernate, but the seeds and dried stems are extremely valuable and are used as a spice.

Elderflower

The important rule when preserving elderflower is to maintain its sweet aroma by not applying heat. Dry it by picking the flowers away from stems, leaving in a thin layer on metal trays at room temperature until dry – this won't work in an overly humid room. Save the stems for infusing into vinegar, oil or cordial.

- For vinegar, leave the stems infusing for at least one month; the more elderflower you pack in, the more intense the flavour will be.
- For oil, leave the stems infusing for at least one month; again, the more elderflower you pack in, the more intense the flavour will be.
- For cordial, boil 5 parts water: 4 parts sugar to dissolve, add 3% citric acid or juiced lemons and let the syrup cool. Pick as many heads of elderflower that will stay submerged in the chilled syrup; leave for 24 hours before straining through a cheese cloth. Store in sterilized jars in the fridge.

Beetroot Prunes

- Steam beetroot, peel, dehydrate at 90°C (194°F) for 20–40 hours until prune-like.
- Hydrate beetroots in a mushroom stock or sour apple juice with 2% salt for 4+ hours.

Salted Cucumbers

Slice cucumbers larger than the intended serving size, to compensate for shrinkage.

- Keep the skin and seeds together, but split the cucumber open to allow proper salting and to expose the seeds.
- Salt the cucumbers generously, then place them individually on ice for 20 minutes.
- Freeze the cucumber overnight, to be defrosted when needed. This process gives the cucumber a unique 'cooked' texture and a flavour similar to oyster.

Brined Tomatoes

Use ripe tomatoes for ease of peeling and, more importantly, to make sure they are porous.

- Whisk 3% sugar and 4% salt into filtered water. Add additional flavours dependent on the dish – herbs, spices, etc.
- Blanch and shock the tomatoes in boiling water and then iced water, to peel them.
- Keep the tomato skins for another purpose, perhaps for jam, dehydration or infusing into spirits.
- Leave the tomatoes in the brine for 1–5 days. They will keep longer, but the texture can become too soft.

Potato Dumplings
- Roast waxy potatoes whole at 200°C (400°F), with full humidity, until tender.
- Remove the skin from the flesh, passing the flesh through a fine sieve.
- Mix flesh with 10% potato starch and 2% salt.
- Form into 2.5cm (1in)-thick torpedo shapes and freeze without stacking, as this will ruin the shape.
- From frozen, deep-fry at 180°C (350°F) until golden brown. Season with salt.

Preserved Gooseberries & Blackberries
In the abundance of the season, pick as many berries as possible at a nice ripe stage.
- Clean the berries by submerging them in water. After 20 minutes, remove any insects that have risen to the surface.
- Freeze and defrost when needed. Of course, the soft defrosted texture is taken into account with the dish, i.e. the dish benefits from the 'cooked' texture.

Mushroom Duxelles
- Cook finely diced shallots in a heavy-based pot with lid until soft and translucent.
- Lightly coat button mushrooms and/or mushroom trimmings and roast at 200°C (400°F) until golden. Chill and finely chop.
- Mix 1 part soft-cooked shallots to 3 parts diced roasted mushrooms.
- Pick individual lemon thyme leaves and add to the cold mushroom mixture to taste.

Braised Kelp
The kelp will impart great flavour into the liquid used here, so have a purpose for the liquid in mind.
- Toast dried kelp in the oven for 4 minutes at 180°C (350°F), then simmer in water or stock until tender.

Black Garlic Paste
Keep whole garlic bulbs in a dehydrator at 60°C (140°F) for 2 weeks, peel and store in the fridge.
- Weigh cauliflower trim to double the weight of the black garlic.
- Steam cauliflower trim until completely soft. Blend with the black garlic until super-smooth.

FERMENTS, PICKLES & PRESERVES

PRESERVING FOOD NATURALLY IS AN ART LOST THROUGH INDUSTRIAL PROCESSING. WHILE PROVIDING ALL THE GOOD BACTERIA, WE TURBOCHARGE THE INGREDIENT WITH PERSONALITY AND DELICIOUSNESS.

LACTO FERMENTS

Other than the Sourdough Miso, Oyster Sauce and the Mushroom 'Papaya' Miso, the following fermentation recipes are done in one of two ways: in a brine or salt rub. They all follow the same methodology, with a few variants of time and salinity:

- Use non-iodized sea salt.
- For a salt rub: add 2% salt to the total mass. Massage the ingredient with the salt until it becomes soft and is leaking moisture, then pack very tightly into a sterilized jar until the liquid covers the ingredient. Roll an unwanted cabbage leaf or other plant scrap to create a plug. The solid mass in the jar should ideally reach up to the brim; the plug should be tightly packed at the top, forcing the liquid above the ingredient.
- For a brine: add 2% of the weight of the ingredient, and the water required to submerge the ingredient.
- Leave at room temperature (ideally 16–18°C/60–64°F) for the desired time. The longer it sits, the more sour the flavour.
- Compost the mouldy cabbage/plant plug and store the ferment in the fridge in a sterilized container.

Fermented Potato Skin & Flesh
- Roast the potatoes whole at 200°C (400°F) with full humidity until tender.
- Remove the skins from the flesh.
- To ferment the skins, pack tightly into an appropriate vessel, covering with a brine as described in Lacto Ferments, above.
- To ferment the flesh, mix with 2% salt then pack in the jar, ensuring there is no oxygen. Let the mix set for 20 minutes in the fridge, pack in a cabbage plug and top with 2.5cm (1in) of 4% brine.
- Leave the skins and the flesh for 2 weeks.

Fermented Swede
- Slice the swedes into 1mm (1/32 in)-thick ribbons – we use a Japanese turning slicer, but a mandolin also works well.
- Ferment in a 2% salt rub as described in Lacto Ferments, above.
- Leave for 10 days.

Fermented Grapes
It's best to use under-ripe grapes because they are firm and have not yet developed their sweetness.
- Ferment in a brine as described in Lacto Ferments, above, but with a 4% salinity.
- Leave for 2 weeks.

Fermented Elderberries
As with grapes, use under-ripe berries.
- Ferment in a brine as described in Lacto Ferments, above, but with a 4% salinity.
- Leave for 2 weeks.

Fermented Fennel
- Slice the fennel into 1mm (1/32 in)-thick strips lengthways with a sharp mandolin.
- Ferment in a 2% salt rub, as described in Lacto Ferments, above.
- Leave for 10 days.

Fermented Onion
- Peel and cut the onions through the centre of the root into two pieces.
- Ferment in a 2% brine, as described in Lacto Ferments, above.
- Leave for 2 weeks.

Fermented Gooseberry
Choose slightly unripe gooseberries.
- Neatly cut off the little gooseberry beards.
- Ferment in a 2% salt rub, as described in Lacto Ferments, above.
- Leave for 1 week.

Sourdough Miso
This product is designed to absorb bread waste, so ideally use what would have otherwise been wasted.
- Soak the bread in water until it's completely soft, then strain the water away so that you are left with the mushy bread pulp.
- Mix with your hands to create an even mush, removing lumps, then mix with equal amounts of koji* and 3% salt of the bread/koji mass.
- Pack into a sterilized jar, ensuring there is no oxygen. Let the mix set for 20 minutes in the fridge, then top with 2.5cm (1in) of 4% brine.

*Koji is made by combining a cultivated mould with rice, soya or other foodstuffs – source from a fellow fermenter or learn how to make your own.

Mushroom 'Papaya' Miso

Select high-protein mushrooms.

- Cook mushrooms over a high heat quickly.
- Cool, then blend with 2% of the enzyme 'papain' and 3.5% salt.
- Place in an airtight container at 40°C (104°F) for a week.

Oyster Sauce

- Blend equal parts oyster meat with mushroom 'papaya' miso.

PICKLE

We use apple cider vinegar, filtered water and light brown sugar in three different ratios:
- 3 parts water: 2 parts vinegar: 2 parts sugar
- 2 parts water: 1 part vinegar: 1 part sugar
- 1 part water: 1 part vinegar: 1 part sugar

Pickled Alexander Stems

- Slice the stems neatly against the grain.
- Weigh the total mass, then add 2% salt and leave for 20 minutes.
- Pour a 3:2:1 pickle (see Pickle, above) over the stems and leave for a minimum of 1 day in the fridge.

Pickled Japanese Knotweed

Pick young, tender shoots.

- Slice the stems neatly against the grain, creating 1mm (½₂ in)-thick discs.
- Weigh the total mass, then add 2% salt and leave for 20 minutes.
- Pour a 3:2:2 pickle (see Pickle, above) over the stems and leave for a minimum of 1 day in the fridge.

Pickled Elderberries

- Clean the elderberries by submerging them in water. After 20 minutes remove any insects that rise to the surface.
- Pour a 3:2:1 pickle (see Pickle, above) over the berries and leave for a minimum of 1 day in the fridge.

Pickled Blackberries & Aronia

Choose under-ripe red blackberries – they are firm and won't turn to mush. Choose aronia when they are firm and not fully developed, again, so they won't turn to mush.

- Wash to clean away any insects and unwanted plant matter.
- In a sterilized jar, submerge the berries in a 2% brine for 1 week in a dark, cool place.
- Separate the berries from the brine, then mix half of the brine with equal parts vinegar and sugar.
- Pour back over the berries and leave in a dark, cool place for between 1 and 2 months, until the berries start to soften.

Pickled Roses

Pick unsprayed rugosa petals – rugosa petals are the best.

- Clean the petals by submerging them in water. After 20 minutes remove any insects that rise to the surface.
- Pour a 1:1:1 pickle (see Pickle, above) over the berries and leave for a minimum of 1 day in the fridge.

Garlic & Elderberry Capers

- Separate berries into individual little spheres.
- Pack into a sterilized jar, covering with salt; elderberry capers for 4 weeks, garlic capers for 6 weeks.
- Rinse thoroughly with water, then place in a sterilized jar and cover with vinegar, leaving for 1 week.

STOCKS, SAUCES & OILS

TO CREATE CLARITY, OUR STOCKS, SAUCES AND OILS ARE EXTREMELY MINIMAL. PURE FLAVOURS REQUIRE MORE ATTENTION, BUT WHEN THE CORRECT HARMONY IS ACHIEVED, THE FOOD IS ALWAYS BETTER.

STOCKS

Mushroom Stock

Use button, chestnut, field and/or any other available mushrooms, including trim.

- Process the mushrooms into thin, uniformed slices/chunks.
- Roast at 220°C (425°F) with full humidity, to prevent burning. Take them out when they are a dark brown colour.
- In an appropriately deep pot, cover the mushrooms with just enough water to submerge them.
- Simmer for 1 hour with the lid on.
- Strain stock through a fine cloth.
- Season, and adjust to taste.

Kelp Stock (savoury)

- As for the mushroom stock, but replace half of the mushrooms with toasted dried kelp.

Kelp Stock (sweet)

- Lightly toast the dried kelp at 160°C (320°F) for 4 minutes.
- In a deep pan, submerge the kelp in filtered water.
- Simmer for 1 hour with the lid on.
- Strain stock through a fine cloth.
- Season, and adjust to taste.

Meat Stock

- Make a stock by roasting the bones until dark golden brown.
- Cover the bones with water and simmer for 8 hours.

Potato Stock

- Roast the potatoes whole at 220°C (425°F) with full humidity, until tender.
- Remove the skin from the flesh, reserving the flesh for another use.
- Place the skins in a dry oven at 120°C (248°F), until bone dry.
- In an appropriately deep pot, cover the skins with just enough water to submerge them.
- Simmer for 1 hour with the lid on.
- Strain stock through a fine cloth.
- Season, and adjust to taste.

SAUCES

Vegetable Treacle

- Collect all edible vegetable scraps.
- Put the scraps in a deep large metal tray, with a small amount of water at the bottom and a lid on top.
- Steam for hours, until the vegetables are complete mush.
- Press the mush through a sieve, collecting all the liquid, then pass the liquid through a muslin cloth.
- Reduce the liquid in a heavy-based pan until the liquid turns to a black treacle.

Beetroot Molasses

- Juice beetroot with the skin on.
- Reduce the liquid in a heavy-based pan until it turns to a sticky glaze.

Fermented Potato Sauce

- Measure 1 part fermented potato flesh with 1 part neutral oil and 2 parts filtered water.
- Blend until smooth.

Kelp/Dulse Sauce

- Measure 1 part fermented potato flesh with 1 part neutral oil and 2 parts kelp stock/dulse.
- Blend until smooth.

Whey Reduction

- Reduce the whey to between half and one-tenth its original volume; the more it reduces, the darker its colour and flavour. Each batch is different, so keep tasting it until it's as you like it and/or it's right for the dish.
- When the whey has reduced by half, pass it through a cloth, as the whey proteins separating at this stage will have an unpleasant texture and bitter flavour. Yoghurt whey doesn't need passing through a cloth.

Buttermilk Reduction

- Process in the same way as whey (above); however, when bringing it to the boil, a curd will separate, so strain this away before reducing.
- Use the curd for another purpose, such as dehydrating and blending into powder.

Mint Sauce
3 parts mint
3 parts vinegar
1 part sugar
- Blend until fine, ensuring that the sugar has dissolved.

Crayfish Sauce
- Roast all your crayfish trim and crayfish you're not using at 180°C (350°F) with a small amount of humidity, until golden brown.
- Cover with filtered water in a deep pot, then infuse for 1 hour.
- Strain, then reduce until the flavour is intense and naturally seasoned.

Pork Sauce
- Reduce pork stock until it starts to slightly thicken.
- Before serving, add an equal mixture of sliced apple and fresh thyme to the sauce, simmer for 20 minutes. The amount of the fresh mixture should be 1:10 the weight of the sauce.
- Pass through a muslin cloth and acidify with dark vinegar.

Blue Cheese Sauce
Select ripe, strong blue cheese.
- Bring 1 part double cream to the boil, take off the heat and whisk in 1 part blue cheese until mostly dissolved.
- Using a hand blender, mix until smooth, but not for too long, otherwise it will split.

Mustard & Mustard Dressing
3 parts mustard powder
3 parts wine, beer or cider (ideally you can utilize surplus/waste)
2 parts mixed (black and yellow) whole mustard seeds
1 part vinegar
2% salt

For the mustard:
- Partially crush the whole mustard seeds, to enable them to absorb the liquid.
- Mix everything and leave for 12 hours.
- Blend half the mixture to a paste, then combine into the same batch.

For the dressing:
- Blend together 2.5 parts neutral oil to 1 part mustard, until glossy.
- Season with salt and vinegar.

Oyster Emulsion
- Shuck the oysters, separating their juice.
- In a blender, add 1 part oyster meat and pour slowly over 2 parts neutral oil, to create a stable emulsion. Add oyster juice if it's too thick – the consistency should be like double cream, not mayonnaise.
- Season with salt and vinegar.

Red Wine Reduction
Use wine that's past its best – this can be white, orange, rosé or red, or even a mixture of the lot.
- Add 20% sugar to the wine.
- In a heavy-based pot, cook until 105°C (221°F) or do the classic jam test – put a drop on a plate to check the consistency. It's important that it's not set, but also not so thin that it will absorb into the food.

Elderberry Reduction
Juice ripe elderberries and compost the pulp.
- Add 70% sugar to the total weight of the juice.
- In a heavy-based pot, cook until 105°C (221°F) or do the classic jam test – put a drop on a plate to check the consistency. It's important that it's not set, but also not so thin that it will absorb into the food.

Parsnip Gravy
- Shred parsnips with the skin on.
- Add a small amount of oil, mix and add to a shallow metal tray not more than 2.5cm/1in deep.
- Roast at 150°C (300°F), mixing every 20 minutes until it is almost burnt.
- Cover with water and leave in the oven for 40 minutes.
- Strain the liquid through a muslin cloth and reduce until strong and slightly thickened.
- Add 0.2% xanthan gum, blend, boil and pass through a fine sieve.

PURÉE

Broccoli / Celeriac / Cauliflower / Pea / Patty Pan / Parsnip

- Shred the vegetable finely in a food processor or a box grater.
- In a heavy-based pot add the vegetable with a little amount of neutral oil and 0.5–1% salt.
- On a medium to high heat, sweat the vegetable until the moisture comes out and then slowly steams away.
- When the pan starts to catch at the base turn the heat to a medium low with the lid on.
- Cook until the vegetable is complete mush.
- Blend into purée, adding a little amount of water and oil just to help it blend.

OILS

Three-Cornered Garlic / Wild Garlic / Marigold / Pineapple Weed / Nasturtium / Fig Leaf / Mint / Alexander / Fennel / Tarragon / Lovage / Basil / Dried Mushroom Oils

- Blend equal parts neutral oil with herb (or mushroom) until the mixture reaches 62°C (144°F). Leave for 12 hours to infuse.
- Pass through a chinois and muslin cloth into an appropriate vessel.

Rosemary / Douglas Fir / Marjoram Oils

Follow the same process (above) but swap 50% of the herb with parsley leaves.

Carrot Top & Garlic / Garlic Oils

Follow the same process (above) but with the addition of 15% garlic to the amount of oil.

Rose / Lemon Thyme / Elderflower Oils

- Pick the leaves/elderflower.
- As soon as possible, lightly pestle-and-mortar the leaves/elderflower to extract the essential oils. Add to an appropriate vessel, then cover in a neutral oil.
- Infuse for at least 24 hours.

Crayfish Oil

- Roast all your crayfish shells (not flesh/moisture) at 180°C (350°F) with a small amount of humidity, until golden brown.
- Crush into an appropriate vessel and cover with a neutral oil for at least 24 hours.

MEAT, FISH & DAIRY

ANIMAL PRODUCTS FROM A NATURAL
SYSTEM ARE EXTREMELY PRECIOUS. WITH
THIS IN MIND WE RECEIVE THESE WHOLE
INGREDIENTS DIRECTLY FROM NATURE AND
PROCESS THEM LOVINGLY FROM SCRATCH.

MEAT

Ageing Meat

When dealing with whole animals, ageing is the key to preserve the meat in its most natural form.

- Upon receiving a whole beast, leave it in a walk-in fridge for a whole week to rest its muscles.
- Break the animal down into its main sections: shoulders, saddle, legs – keeping the bones in place.
- Cover the whole beast thoroughly in rendered fat, which can be obtained by rendering the excess fat from previous beasts. The rotation goes on and on.
- Cracks will appear in the fat, especially if the section gets moved around. It's very important to cover all these gaps, ensuring there is no oxygen touching the flesh, as this would ruin the meat.

Braising Meat

- Select the braising cuts of the aged animal, trim and cut into appropriate sizes.
- Take an equal weight in onions as you have meat, peel, thinly slice and cook in a heavy-based pot with 1% salt. Cook the onions slowly with a lid on, until very soft. Take off the lid and caramelize until golden.
- Make a braising stock from the same animal, season the stock with 0.5–1% salt.
- Grill the meat at a high heat to gain as much dark brown colouration as possible.
- Add the meat and onions to an appropriate braising tray with the stock just covering the meat. Put a lid on the tray and place in a combination oven at 200°C (400°F) with full humidity for 40 minutes. Then turn it down to 120°C (248°F) and cook until the meat is soft – this will vary depending on the size of the meat.
- Cool the whole tray down quickly with the lid off, but the meat still submerged in the stock.

Braising Juices

- Strain the stock through muslin cloth and reduce until slightly thickened, then cut with dark vinegar.
- Thicken with 0.1% xanthan gum.

Roasting Meat

- Select the primary cuts of the aged animal.
- Trim, clean and portion the meat to an appropriate size.
- Bring to room temperature.
- Grill the meat at a high temperature to gain as much dark caramelization as possible, then cook slowly at a lower temperature until the internal temperature reaches 52–56°C (125–133°F), depending on the animal.
- After the meat has rested (and resting juices collected), slice and season with 0.5–1% salt.

Resting Juices

- When the meat is resting in a bowl, pour a small amount of stock made from the same animal over the meat to collect resting juices and make a sauce.
- Pass through muslin cloth and thicken with 0.1% xanthan gum.

Blood Cake

Spice mix
2 parts nutmeg
2 parts black pepper
1 part star anise
1 part cinnamon
1 part clove
- Grind into fine powder freshly before use.

Blood cake
4 parts blood
1 part soft caramelized onions (light golden brown colour)
1 part cured pork back fat
0.5% salt

- Dice the fat into neat 1cm (⅜in) cubes.
- Cook blood in a heavy-based pan on a low heat until the temperature reaches 62°C (144°F), then take off the heat and add the other ingredients.
- Once evenly mixed, pour into an appropriately sized tray lined with greaseproof paper – the mix should be at least 4cm (1¾in) thick.
- Cook in a steam oven set at 90°C (194°F) until the internal temperature reaches 85°C (185°F).
- Chill quickly, then cut to weight.

Poaching Pork
- Make a pork stock, add 2% salt and keep at 64°C (147°F) – this can be done in an oven, carefully on the stove or in a waterbath.
- Select the primary cuts of the aged pig, trim, portion and bring to room temperature.
- Poach the portions of pig until the internal temperature reaches 58°C (136°F), then turn it down to 56°C (133°F) and hold at that temperature for 30 minutes before serving.

Cured Pork
- Cure the belly in 20% salt, 15% sugar and 0.5% saltpetre for 1 week, turning every day.
- Rinse thoroughly, dry and hang.

FISH

Processing Fish
Separate the fish into fillets, offal, skin, head and bones. We cure the fillets for cooking or serving raw, make stock from the bones, turn the eggs/roe into caviar and the rest goes into making fish sauce/garum.

Curing Fish
- Combine salt and sugar to the ratio of 60 salt to 40 sugar.
- Cover all the flesh with a layer of this curing mix for 30 minutes.
- If the skin is on the flesh, add slightly more mix. Fish such as mackerel and gurnard benefit from the skin becoming easier to peel.

Caviar
You can make caviar from any fish eggs (also known as roe).
- Carefully remove the membrane and wash the eggs in cold water, then allow to drip-dry.
- Add 2–3% salt, then add to a sterilized container, ensuring there's no trapped air.
- Age the caviar to develop the flavour.

DAIRY

Sour Cream
- In a heavy-based pan, slowly heat the cream to 80°C (176°F), then take it off the heat.
- When the cream falls to 45°C (113°F), add 15% previous batch live sour cream or cultured buttermilk.
- Keep the cream mixture at 38°C (100°F) for 6–8 hours, then chill the sour cream quickly.

Butter
- Add sour cream to a kitchen mixer with a K paddle or whisk attachment.
- Mix on medium to high speed, making sure you manage the splattering.
- The sour cream will first become whipped cream, then it will slowly start to separate – keep mixing until it is noticeably butter.
- Squeeze the butter with your hands, making sure you separate all the buttermilk.
- Mix 2% salt to the butter.
- Reserve the buttermilk for culturing.

Cultured Buttermilk
If you made butter from normal cream (not cultured), then you can still culture the buttermilk as you would make sour cream.
- Add 15% previous batch cultured buttermilk or live yoghurt.
- Keep the mixture at 38°C (100°F) for 6–8 hours, then chill the buttermilk quickly.

Yoghurt
- In a heavy-based pan, slowly heat milk to 80°C (176°F), then take it off the heat.
- When the milk falls to 45°C (113°F), add 15% previous batch live yoghurt.
- Hold the temperature of the pan at 38°C (100°F) for 6–8 hours, then chill the yoghurt quickly.
- If you want the yoghurt to be thicker, add milk powder at the same stage as you add the live yoghurt. You can also strain the yoghurt through a muslin cloth, collecting the whey for other use.

Curd
- In a heavy-based pan, heat 4 parts milk and 1 part cream up to 80°C (176°F), remove from the heat and add 2% acid in the form of rennet, lemon juice or vinegar. Stir the liquids together.
- After 30 minutes the curds and the whey should start to separate.
- Gently pour the mixture through a muslin cloth and leave in the fridge for 3 hours, or until the curd is how you like it.
- Keep the whey for other use.

Dehydrated Yoghurt
- Dry yoghurt at 90°C (194°F) in a combination oven with 0% humidity until dry and golden brown.

NUTS, GRAINS, SEEDS & SWEET THINGS

WHILE SEEDS, NUTS AND GRAINS PLAY SMALL ROLES, THEY BRING BIG PLEASURE, ESPECIALLY WITH THE SWEET THINGS.

Walnut Butter
- Toast walnuts in an oven at 160°C (320°F), until a light golden brown.
- When cool, blend until smooth and add vinegar and salt to taste.

Walnut Praline
- In an appropriate-sized deep pan, cover walnuts with a neutral oil and cook on a medium to low heat until the inside of the nut is a light gold brown – test this by snapping a nut in two.
- When the mix is cool, separate the oil then chop the nuts neatly, until they are the consistency of a fine granola.
- Finish by adding a touch of the oil back over the grain to bind it together, seasoning with vinegar and salt.

Pumpkin Seed Praline
- In an appropriate-sized deep pan, cover pumpkin seeds with a neutral oil and cook on a medium to low heat until the inside of the seed is a light gold brown – test this by snapping a seed in two.
- When the mix is cool, separate the oil, then chop the seeds neatly, until they are the consistency of a fine granola.
- Finish by adding a touch of the oil back over the grain to bind it together, seasoning with vinegar and salt.

Caramelized Cacao Shells
- In a thick-based pan, make a hard ball caramel to 120°C (248°F), with 2 parts demerara sugar and 1 part water.
- Add triple the volume of cacao shells, mix, then lay thin on greaseproof mats, with plenty of space in between the shells.
- Once set, rebake in the oven at 180°C (350°F) until the excess caramel separates and you get finer pieces of cacao shell.

Pumpkin Seed Butter
- On a large flat tray, roast the pumpkin seeds until they become a light gold brown.
- When the seeds are cool, blend into a thick smooth paste.
- Finish by seasoning with vinegar and salt.

Hazelnut Butter
- On a large flat tray roast the hazelnuts until they become a light gold brown.
- When the nuts are cool, blend into a thick smooth paste.
- Finish by seasoning with vinegar and salt.

Oat Paste
- Mix 2 parts freshly rolled oats, 1 part butter, 1 part sugar. This should be made no more than a few hours before serving.
- Melt sugar and butter in a pan, add the oats to the pan and mix thoroughly, adding salt to taste.
- Lay on greaseproof mats and bake in thin layers at 160°C (320°F) until golden.
- Squash the mixture into a deep metal container and keep in a warm place to prevent it setting.

Caramelized Oats
- In a thick-based pan, make a hard ball caramel to 120°C (248°F), with 2 parts demerara sugar and 1 part water.
- Add triple the volume of freshly rolled oats, mix, then lay thin on greaseproof mats with plenty of space.
- Once set, rebake in the oven at 180°C (350°F) until the excess caramel separates and you get finer clusters of oats.

Linseed Brittle
- Over a set of scales, pour 3 times the weight of boiling water over the linseeds.
- Weigh 10% potato starch and 1% salt to the total mass of linseed mix.
- Mix and leave for 20 minutes.
- Spread thinly on greaseproof mats.
- Bake at 150°C (300°F) until dry and crispy.

Miso Caramel
- Mix 3 parts demerara sugar, 1 part water, 2 parts cream and miso, to taste.
- In a thick-based pan, make a hard ball caramel to 120°C (248°F) with sugar and water.
- Take off the heat, add the cream, chill to room temperature and season with miso.

Malt Toffee

Melt 1 part dark brown sugar and 1 part butter together in a pan until the sugar dissolves, then add 1 part malt syrup.

Cacao toffee

Melt 2 parts dark brown sugar and 2 parts butter together in a pan until the sugar dissolves, then add 1 part blended cacao shells with the consistency of semolina.

Caramelized Honey

Cook the honey in a heavy-based pot until it starts to smell a little burnt and turns a dark golden brown colour.

Sea Buckthorn Jelly

Equal parts sea buckthorn juice and water
35% sugar
1% bronze gelatine
- Soak gelatine in cold water for 5 minutes.
- Dissolve the gelatine and sugar in a small amount of the sea buckthorn liquid, add to the rest of the mix.
- Strain through a fine sieve into the desired moulds.
- Set in the fridge.

Poached Gooseberries

Select slightly under-ripe gooseberries.
- Mix 1 part gooseberries with 80% wine, 70% sugar and 10% pineapple weed (this can be foraged).
- Whisk to dissolve the sugar.
- Poach at 72°C (162°F) for 5 minutes.

Frozen Sea Buckthorn

- Mix equal parts water to sea buckthorn juice with 10% sugar.
- Whisk to dissolve the sugar, then freeze and scrape into granita.

Frozen Pineapple Weed

- Melt 1 part sugar in 4 parts water.
- Chill, then add 1 part pineapple weed.
- Steep overnight, strain, freeze and scrape into granita.

Frozen Greengage

- Add 10% sugar to greengage plum juice.
- Dissolve, freeze and scrape into granita.

Frozen Elderberry

- Add 10% sugar to elderberry juice.
- Acidify to taste, dissolve, freeze and scrape into granita.

Frozen Sour Cream

- Heat the sour cream, sweeten with 10% caramelized honey and add 1% salt.
- Freeze, then break into small clusters, approximately 2cm (¾in) thick.

Saffron Cream

- Bring double cream to a simmer in a heavy-based pot.
- Remove from the heat and add 1% saffron. Leave for 30 minutes.
- When it is chilled, whip into a soft pillow-like consistency.

Brown Butter Solids

- Weigh out equal parts of butter and milk powder.
- Melt the butter in a heavy-based pot and add the milk powder.
- On a low to medium heat, slowly caramelize the mixture, stirring to prevent it catching on the bottom.
- When it starts to bubble, add a small amount of water, which will cause the mix to boil briefly.
- Stir minimally, but still prevent the bottom from catching until the fats and the solids separate.
- Once there is clear separation, turn the heat to medium, stirring as normal.
- Once the mixture is golden brown, strain through a muslin cloth, reserving the liquid butter for another use.

CORDIALS

Elderflower / Fig Leaf / Alexander Leaf
- Boil 5 parts of water with 4 parts sugar to dissolve, add 3% citric acid and let the syrup cool.
- Pick young fig and alexander leaves. Pick the elderflowers when they are freshly open.
- Submerge the flowers/leaves as much as you can in the chilled syrup. Leave for 24 hours before straining through a cheese cloth.
- Store in sterilized jars in the fridge.

PUFF PASTRY

Dough
1 part wholewheat freshly milled flour
1 part strong white flour
1 part cold filtered water

6% room butter (room temperature)
3% white wine vinegar
3% fresh yeast

Additional butter
50% weight of the final dough. This should be pressed into 2cm (¾in) square slabs, then used at room temperature. Depending on the scale of your batch, you don't want to create square slabs bigger than 40cm (16in) wide, as they would be too difficult to work with.

- Mix the dough ingredients together in a mixer, excluding the additional butter. It is important that the dough becomes tight, but not to the stage where it tears.
- Rest the dough in a neat ball in the fridge for at least 1 hour.
- On a well-floured surface, shape the dough into a square, then create four equal 'ears'. These ears will serve as flaps to wrap the additional butter. The four ears should be the same volume as the central part of the dough; this is done by eye – bear in mind the ears will be rolled into square shapes.

- With a rolling pin, roll the ears and the centre out as wide as the slab of butter; the ears will be much thinner than the centre. The final shape should be like a squared cross, with each square having square corners. It is important that both the butter and dough are the same temperature.
- Add the slab of butter directly into the centre of the cross, which should not hang over the edge.
- Fold the ears over the slab of butter to create a neat parcel. Be mindful of excess flour at this stage – you want the dough to stick together and excess flour will prevent this. There should be no butter exposed, it should all be neatly tucked inside.
- Carefully roll the square slab evenly into a rectangle three times its original length – no butter should escape. Fold this long rectangle into 3 equal parts, creating the original shape. Put it in the fridge to rest for 30 minutes.
- Repeat the last step three times, resting in the fridge between each roll. Each time, twist the dough 90° to roll it in a different direction, creating neat, uniformed layers of butter.
- Finally, roll the dough to 1cm (⅜in) thick, trimming the edges to create a uniformed shape, which is important for an accurate cooking time.

Cooking programme
210°C (410°F) / 10 minutes / 20% dry humidity
180°C (350°F) / 20 minutes / 20% dry humidity
160°C (320°F) / 40 minutes / 20% dry humidity
140°C (284°F) / 20 minutes / 20% dry humidity
120°C (248°F) / 20 minutes / 20% dry humidity
110°C (230°F) / 20 minutes / 20% dry humidity

ICE CREAMS & SORBETS

WE LOVE ICE CREAM, ALMOST TO THE POINT WHERE WE WANT EVERY DESSERT TO BE ICE CREAM. ICE CREAM SHOULDN'T BE A SMALL ELEMENT OF A DISH, IT'S THE STAR OF THE SHOW AND DESERVES ALL THE ATTENTION.

ICE CREAM

Alexander & Cacao Butter Ice Cream
Cacao butter
2 parts cacao butter
0.5 parts neutral oil

Alexander milk base
8 parts water
2 parts alexander leaf

5% glucose
2% dextrose
1% glycerine
0.2% salt

Alexander cordial
4 parts alexander leaf cordial

- Blanch, refresh and squeeze the alexander leaf so there's no excess liquid.
- Blend the water, glucose, salt and alexander until smooth and the sugars totally melt. Strain through a fine sieve.
- Mix the cordial with the mixture and keep warm, around 50°C (120°F).
- Melt the cacao butter with the oil over a bain marie.
- Emulsify the two mixtures at the same temperature using a hand blender.
- Churn.

Pumpkin Seed Ice Cream
Pumpkin seed milk
8 parts water
2 parts sugar
1 part toasted pumpkin seeds

3% raisins
3% glucose
1% salt

Pumpkin seed butter
3 parts toasted pumpkin seeds

- Toast the pumpkin seeds for both the milk and butter to a light golden colour.
- Let the seeds cool down, then blend the butter in a blender until smooth – this won't need any liquid, just the natural oils.
- Blend the water, sugar, glucose, salt and seeds until smooth. The sugars will totally melt. Strain through a fine sieve.
- Mix the milk and butter together, churn.

Sourdough Ice Cream
5 parts milk
3 parts sour cream
1 part sugar
1 part fine breadcrumbs

7% glucose
0.3% salt

- Heat the milk, sour cream, glucose and sugar up to 80°C (176°F). Take the pan off the heat.
- Toast the breadcrumbs in an oven at 160°C (320°F) until they are a dark brown colour.
- Add to the hot liquid to infuse for 1 hour.
- Strain out half of the breadcrumbs.
- Add salt and churn.

Pine & Algae Ice Cream
4 parts pine nuts
2 parts kelp stock
1 part sugar

5% glucose
2% dextrose
1% glycerine
0.5% chlorella
0.2% salt

- Toast the pine nuts to a light golden colour.
- Blend the seeds in a blender until smooth, this won't require any liquid, just the natural oils.
- Blend the kelp stock with the other ingredients until the sugars melt, strain through a fine sieve and mix with the butter.
- Mix the milk and butter together, churn.

Raw Cream Ice Cream
5 parts raw sour cream
3 parts raw milk
1 part sugar

7% glucose
0.5 % salt

Use really fresh, well-processed raw dairy.
- Make the sour cream but with raw cream.
- Heat just 1 part of the raw milk up to 80°C (176°F), then add the glucose and sugar.
- Take off the heat, chill to room temperature, add the raw sour cream and salt, then churn.

Fig Leaf & Cacao Butter Ice Cream

Cacao butter
2 parts cacao butter
0.5 parts neutral oil

Seed milk base
8 parts water
1 part toasted pumpkin seeds

7% glucose
3% dried dates
3% dried fig leaf powder
0.2% chlorella
0.2% salt

Fig leaf cordial
4 parts fig leaf cordial

- Toast the pumpkin seeds to a light golden colour.
- Blend the water, dates, glucose, salt, chlorella and toasted seeds until smooth and the sugars totally melt. Strain through a fine sieve.
- Mix the cordial with the seed milk and keep warm, around 50°C (120°F).
- Melt the cacao butter with the oil over a bain marie.
- Emulsify the two mixtures at the same temperature using a hand blender.
- Churn.

Sheep's/Goat's Cheese Ice Cream

5 parts milk
3 parts sour cream
3 parts strong sheep's/goat's cheese
2 parts sugar

5% glucose

It's crucial to use a ripe, strong, pungent cheese – the strength of the cheese defines the recipe, so adapt it as necessary.
- Cut the cheese into small pieces.
- Heat the milk, sour cream, glucose, cheese and sugar up to 80°C (176°F).
- Take off the heat and blend.
- Chill and churn.

Elderflower & Cacao Butter Ice Cream

Cacao butter
2 parts cacao butter
0.5 parts elderflower oil

Seed milk base
8 parts water
1 part toasted pumpkin seeds

3% dried dates
7% glucose
0.5% salt
4 parts elderflower cordial

- Toast the pumpkin seeds to a light golden colour.
- Blend the water, dates, glucose, salt and toasted seeds until smooth and the sugars totally melt. Strain through a fine sieve.
- Mix the cordial with the seed milk and keep warm, around 50°C (120°F).
- Melt the cacao butter with the oil over a bain marie.
- Emulsify the two mixtures at the same temperature using a hand blender.
- Churn.

Malt Ice Cream

6 parts milk
3 parts sour cream
2 parts malted barley
1 part sugar

5% glucose
0.5% salt

- Heat the milk, sour cream, glucose and sugar up to 80°C (176°F).
- Take off the heat and add the malt barley.
- Add salt, then churn.

Saffron Ice Cream

5 parts milk
3 parts sour cream
1 part sugar

7% glucose
0.2% salt
0.1% saffron

- Heat the milk, sour cream, glucose and sugar up to 80°C (176°F).
- Take off the heat and add saffron.
- Add salt, then churn.

Potato Skin Ice Cream
Potato milk
8 parts water
2 parts sugar
1 part toasted pumpkin seeds

3% raisins
3% glucose
1% salt

Potato skin butter
3 parts roasted potato skin
Neutral oil

This recipe is best done with small, slowly grown potatoes with thick skin.
- Roast the potatoes whole at 200°C (400°F) with full humidity until tender.
- Remove the skin from the flesh – depending on the size of the potato, it's likely to have more flesh than you need. Do not leave any flesh on the skins, as this will negatively affect the skin butter. Reserve the remaining flesh for another use.
- Blend the skins, adding just enough neutral oil so that the skin blends into a thick smooth paste.
- Blend the water, sugar, glucose and salt until the sugars melt. Add the flesh and blend briefly until smooth. Be careful not to blend too long or the mix will become starchy. Strain through a fine sieve.
- Mix the milk and butter together, churn.

Miso Ice Cream
5 parts milk
3 parts sour cream
1 part sugar

7% glucose
4% savoury miso

It's crucial to adapt the recipe to the miso – this recipe is based on an aggressive, salty, savoury miso.
- Heat the milk, sour cream, glucose and sugar up to 80°C (176°F).
- Take off the heat and blend the miso in with a hand blender.
- Chill and churn.

FRUIT SORBETS

Rhubarb / Red Gooseberry / Blackcurrant / Rosehip

4 parts fruit
1 part water
1 part light brown sugar

5% glucose
2% dextrose
1% glycerine
0.5% salt

Rhubarb
- Steam the rhubarb until completely soft, then cool it down as fast as possible.
- Blend with the sorbet ingredients until fine, pass through a sieve and churn.

Red Gooseberry
- Wash then remove the little beards and any stems that might be attached.
- Blend with the sorbet ingredients until fine, pass through a sieve and churn.

Blackcurrant
- Wash, then remove the little beards and any stems that might be attached.
- Blend with the sorbet ingredients until fine, pass through a sieve and churn.

Rosehip
- Wash, then remove the stems and seeds.
- Freeze then defrost the rosehip to give a soft 'cooked' texture.
- Blend with the sorbet ingredients until fine, pass through a sieve and churn.

4

NO
CONCLUSION

WASTE IS A HUMAN THING

HUMAN NATURE IS AN ANOMALY. THE RISE OF HUMANS COULD BE VIEWED IN VERY DIFFERENT WAYS – TRANSCENDING INTO GODS OR PERHAPS A VIRUS UPON EARTH.

Waste is something we created, it's a symptom of our flawed system. However, nature is a perfect system – in nature there is no waste.

And what makes us different from every other species on Earth? We discovered fire, which gave us the ability to do what no other animal can – cook.

We evolved into self-aware conscious beings. This could have been from eating magic mushrooms, a valid hypothesis. We're hunter-gatherers by nature – we could have easily been eating magic 'shrooms, developing this out-of-mind perspective.

This is the second human anomaly – our imagination. No other species has an imagination.

And then, through advanced communication we created today's world, with all its plastic, pollution and waste. And that's the rise of the humans. It's ironic that our imagination is the cause of so much destruction; furthermore, that cooking is the cause of this book.

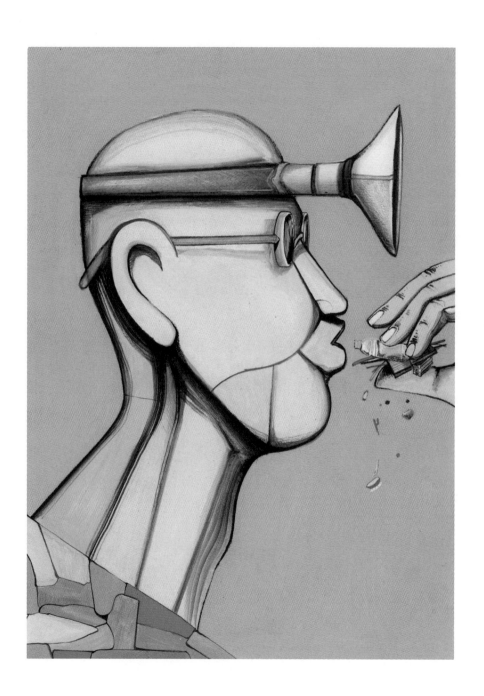

ALL IS MACHINE

YOU KNOW THE EXPRESSION 'YOU CAN'T SEE THE WOOD FOR THE TREES'? WE'RE BORN INTO A WOOD MADE OF STEEL, PLASTIC AND RUBBER – WELCOME TO THE MACHINE.

We're so accustomed to the machine, we can't see it for what it really is.

Our landscape is industrial, our agriculture is industrial, our behaviour and culture is moulded by industrialism. Processed food is not alive, we are alive, we're on a planet which is alive; it doesn't make sense to eat dead food.

Industrialism brings humans prosperity – wealth, luxury, convenience, choice. It sends us into space and saves lives.

It's a brilliant idea, like capitalism…The problem with both these ideas is greed. When greed enters the equation, the system fails.

If processed food didn't make anyone rich, it wouldn't exist.

We are part of nature, but we act like we are above nature: we manipulate it to our advantage with little understanding of the consequences. We know so much less than we accept, and our crude understanding of nature breaks nature.

CHANGE IS HARD

HUMAN BEHAVIOUR IS A POWERFUL FORCE. WE CONFORM IN THE FOOTSTEPS OF OTHERS, OFTEN WITHOUT RATIONALIZATION.

We like to think of ourselves as individual, but we are all connected; we dance in swarms, we get aggressive in mobs, we feel atmosphere and are more intuitive and intelligent in swarms – this is the 'hive mind'.

Humans think like a hive, we conform to a way of doing, a way of thinking, a way of accepting, a way of knowing, a way of desiring.

When you try to explain to the next human that we are doing something bad, they agree, 'Yeah, of course this is bad', but because it's practised by the greater majority of humans, it's acceptable. Opposing the hive's behaviour meets great resistance. For one human to try and change the way of the hive is improbable, but not impossible.

When you stand against the hive, no matter how justified and worthy the cause, 'there will be blood'.

ADD BEAUTY

SINCE HUMAN CONSCIOUSNESS, HOW MUCH DESTRUCTION HAVE WE IMPARTED ON THE EARTH? THE MORE WE WANT, THE MORE NATURE SUFFERS.

We choose to gaze at positive things and avoid the negative; there's no penalty for ignoring the problem. How many people think about landfill sites as they dump waste, or think about animal slaughter when eating cheap meat?

The big cultural problem with industrialism is apathy. We're detached from nature, rendering it a commodity – it's expendable.

Concrete landscapes could harness life, not crush it; invasive species could be in supermarkets; plastic could become art; organic food could just be 'food'.

Humans have scarred the earth, there's no question – in the future that scar can serve as a reminder.

Imagine if organic farming made you famous, rather than reality TV. If that was the world we lived in, we would have a healthy planet. Nature would prosper, not just humans.

Shine light through the broken places, make that which is unappetizing delicious. Make that which is ugly glow. Make that which is ethical sexy. To let heal, to reconfigure, to restore order to the earth … Live and let live.

BREED INTUITION

INTUITION IS A NEGLECTED GIFT PURGED FROM TWENTIETH-CENTURY EDUCATION.

Our education has been a factory line, carbon-copying information for robot thinking.

An industrial system breeds industrial thinking; all the vectors of consistency point to the machine.

The opposite to industrial thinking is intuition. Intuition is the natural way of thinking.

Nature is never the same twice; this inconsistency requires adaptability. There are limitless problems in the world. If we think like a machine we only find ourselves with the same problems. The problems are there because we haven't adapted a solution; the only way to find a solution is to think outside the machine.

This thinking is necessary to a natural food system.

There are no two vegetables that are the same, no two days of cooking that are the same, no two humans that are the same. Industrial systems give us the same ingredients every day, through all the seasons. When you only put square shapes in square spaces, you don't understand the circle.

Your thinking becomes linear and you can't adapt.

When you adapt, your mind is able to make connections and find solutions to the unpredictable nature of real food.

CREATIVITY WILL SAVE US?

HUMANS ARE THE ONLY SPECIES WITH IMAGINATION; WE ARE CAPABLE OF ABSTRACT THOUGHT.

Penguins don't visit art galleries and goats don't foster concepts. However, it's important to state, goats and penguins don't destroy the planet, it's only humans that do. To blame our imagination for global destruction – it's certainly a big part of the puzzle.

Being creative is just the brain connecting information. A synthesis of thoughts found commonly in those willing to be changed.

When you connect unfamiliar pieces of information, your instincts ring like a metal detector. You've found an idea.

Creativity is harmonious with intuition, two peas in a pod, yin and yang. Intuition is adaptivity and creativity is openness.

People don't change the world, ideas do.

Not being creative is like wearing blinkers: you're forced to see only what's in front of you. Without the blinkers, your mind opens, you can look up, seeing the information like a constellation.

Creativity alone will not answer the world's problems; however, it is our best chance for ecological redemption.

PERFECTION DOES NOT EXIST

A HUMAN DESIRE, AN ILLUSION BORN FROM STORIES, PERFECTION IS A TOXIC CONCEPT THAT ENCOURAGES DISCRIMINATION AND CREATES INEQUALITY.

Gastronomy is plagued with perfection. These delusions result in mountains of waste. The term 'primary ingredients' denominates ingredients as secondary or by-products, which suggests that product is less than perfect – and so the waste mounts.

The whole industry puts perfection to the top of its agenda, ethics are only an afterthought.

Humans tell stories, stories that other humans believe, and so we live in these imagined worlds with hypothetical meaning. We believe in religion, we believe in law, we believe in these things that aren't actually real. They're just stories that humans have told.

And through those stories we've believed in this idea of perfection. It's a pyramid and we should all climb to the summit.

Climbing to the top is toxic. It breeds a selfish, superficial standard that is damaging psychologically and socially – to the world, to culture, to the people around you.

Work to a different standard: brilliant is enough. Ten chefs can spend 10 hours mimicking the shape of a sunflower on a plate. Or 10 chefs could spend 10 hours growing a field of sunflowers.

We can be brilliant without compromise; less time engineering meaningless fluff, more time doing things with real value. It's a natural standard that nature can entertain, and nature can entertain brilliance everywhere.

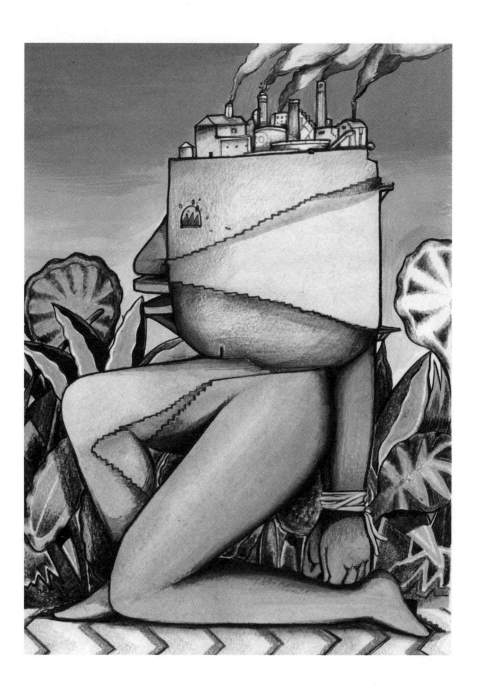

PERSPECTIVE IS A BEAUTIFUL THING

WITH A PROBLEM LIKE WASTE, IT'S NATURAL TO LOOK CLOSELY AND SEE ONLY THE FINER DETAILS.

When you step back and see the bigger picture – why waste exists and where it comes from – you can see the patterns rather than the details. It's not always a pretty perspective, but it's a crucial one.

When you step back and look at the last 200 years, you see that we have gone from a decentralized farm-to-table system to a centralized farm-to-factory system. These patterns correlate with a number of other patterns, such as pollution, food intolerance, man-made diseases, a rise in global warming, degradation of soil fertility, decreased biodiversity and exhaustion of fossil fuels.

Seeing information through patterns makes the cause stick out like a sore thumb. The correlation between industrialism and nature's demise is crystal clear.

While the patterns reveal our destruction they also reveal the infancy of our destructive behaviour. Like a child learning to walk, it's just a matter of time until we find our balance. In a thousand years from now we might consider this an ecological trip, growing pains on the path to Valhalla.

DON'T FORGET TO SMELL THE FLOWERS

TODAY'S WORLD IS A COMPLICATED REALM POLLUTED WITH INFORMATION.

We get overwhelmed because our minds can only understand a fraction of this data, and so we switch off. The best way to deal with waste is with positive rational attention. It's less important that waste exists; what is important is how we react.

We like what we understand, and fear what we don't – we don't understand waste so we tolerate it, considering it a necessary part of our existence. It's only existed for a tiny fraction of history, it's not necessary, it's just something we've ignored, until now.

Dealing with other humans' ignorance is less than attractive, unless you shift your perspective. See failure as an opportunity. Let go of the cynicism, being negative is a bad strategy.

All life is just a mass of cells, positive and negative energy, crashing against each other. The meaning we derive from the world is just our own kind of illusion, it's just a story. It doesn't matter, nothing we do matters, only when we decide it matters.

It's a steadying acceptance to all that we create and all that we break.

Make peace with human failure, it's inevitable. Everything isn't going to be OK, but you're not responsible for that which is out of your hands. All you can do is make what *is* in your hands positive.

Being overwhelmed means we're stuck at a red light; making peace with this existence means we can move forward through a green light.

ZERO WASTE IS NATURE

TO ACHIEVE ZERO WASTE IS TO INTEGRATE WITH NATURE. IT HAS EVERYTHING WE DESIRE AND THERE NEEDS TO BE NO COMPROMISE.

This series of conclusions began with the acknowledgement of why waste exists – humans. I'd like to 'conclude' with how waste could cease to exist.

If we want something, the answer is in nature. If we want a natural plastic equivalent, there's a superior natural alternative – we just haven't found it yet. If we want to feed 10 billion people with natural food, we just need to change our thinking. The systems highlighted in this book are not hypothetical – they exist. Furthermore, they will flourish the more that similar systems of equal integrity flourish.

People who believe that industrialism is the only way to feed the world are short-sighted muppets who can't see the bigger picture. I know this because they all said that Silo couldn't work. It works brilliantly – one giant pre-industrial leap back to the future of food, back to nature, to the land without a bin.

A natural food system cannot create waste, because everything is natural: Zero Waste is nature.

A ZERO WASTE GLOSSARY

blueprint A guide, a design, a pattern to be followed. Silo is the blueprint for the future.

closed loop System that perpetually feeds back into itself.

compost The linchpin of the closed-loop Zero Waste system; all biodegradable leftovers can be thrown into the pot, which then feeds back into the soil to grow the next harvest.

cradle to cradle Not recycling; choosing materials that live productive, long lives, which can be reborn into something new that can ultimately feed back into the system.

direct trade The most important part of a Zero Waste system. When you trade with nature there's no packaging. Generates respect; the food is 'more alive', there is little/no waste, greater transparency, better quality and improved economical margins.

ethicalism Behaving, thinking, acting ethically; idealistic devotion to all things ethical. The reality of being ethical is championing ethical activities to the limit of what you can sustain.

fermenting Antidote to processed industrial food. Ancient form of preservation that harnesses the unseen world of bacteria to bring us physiological gut well-being.

foraging Offers far more than culinary wild treats – it's a connection to nature.

indirect trade Created by industrialism, which drives division between origin and consumer. Causes massive quantities of waste food. The consumer is detached from nature, food culture changes, resulting in apathy.

industrial food system Produces food that we want, not need, and that's always the same. Relies on large-scale agriculture, storage, processing, transportation and retail processes, and the middleman. Unsustainably forces nature to do what benefits humans.

industrialism The reason for human prosperity, but also massive creator of waste. Wraps our food in packaging, creating more waste.

Jedi cooking The cooking method adopted by Silo; encourages and harnesses intuition.

middleman Means processing and packaging: buys food from the farmer, processes it, packages it, holds it in convenient locations and then distributes it to the consumer. Why waste exists and why the natural integrity of food is lost.

paleo Primal hunter-gatherer diet, pre-agriculture.

pre-industrial food system Ethical farming practices, when animals lived symbiotically with humans and humans took only what they needed from nature.

processed food Dead food devoid of real taste, nutrients and natural bacteria; a product of industry.

real food Tastes better, unpredictable, alive, from nature.

recycling Industrial process built to tackle waste, which itself creates various forms of waste: material, time, energy, space, money.

rewilding Low-carbon, slow-farming way of returning exhausted arable land to natural productivity, allowing nature to take control.

Silo A statement; pro-agriculture; a means to legitimize the natural system.

Silo food formula The Silo hypothesis – Zero Waste – in the flesh; a generator of new food.

vegan No animal products; motivated by the unethical reality of the dairy and meat industries. Silo champions a new wave of vegan food, with quality as a priority.

waste Something humans created; a symptom of our flawed system. One man's waste is another man's treasure.

wild food The most nutritious food of all, foraged and cooked in the way nature intends.

Zero Waste To work only with natural materials, letting everything live its life then return to nature. A web of nature, everything is connected. The future of food.

INDEX

ACKNOWLEDGEMENTS

Author acknowledgements

This book has taken nearly five years to create and marks ten years from its original motivation. My motivation to make Silo exist is because of Joost Bakker; Silo was his idea, his vision and so I do what I do in honour of his genius.

We are moulded by our environment, our experiences and mostly by people – friends, family, foes and even people we don't know.

I'm sure most of my staff would describe me as difficult, or perhaps an unpredictable force of chaos. This is probably true and this is why I would like to say thank you, I love you and I'm very sorry, for everything. This book exists because you had faith in my vision – you held the ship together as the storms nearly destroyed us.

A special thanks to David for gambling on me and never trying to compromise what we stand for.

Lastly thanks to Dan and Claire, Claire you're the mother of Silo and Dan you're a Jedi knight, the chosen one.